How to Deal With Your
Self-Destruct Button

How to Deal With Your Self-Destruct Button

Identifying the Lunatic Gene

Adam Shaw

WHITE OWL
AN IMPRINT OF PEN & SWORD BOOKS LTD.
YORKSHIRE – PHILADELPHIA

First published in Great Britain in 2021 by
White Owl
An imprint of Pen & Sword Books Ltd
Yorkshire - Philadelphia

ISBN 9781526779052

Typeset in INDIA By IMPEC eSolutions

Printed and bound in the UK by CPI Group (UK) Ltd., Croydon, CR0 4YY

Pen & Sword Books Ltd. incorporates the Imprints of Pen & Sword Books
Archaeology, Atlas, Aviation, Battleground, Discovery, Family History,
History, Maritime, Military, Naval, Politics, Railways, Select, Transport,
True Crime, Fiction, Frontline Books, Leo Cooper, Praetorian Press,
Seaforth Publishing, Wharncliffe and White Owl.

For a complete list of Pen & Sword titles please contact

PEN & SWORD BOOKS LIMITED
47 Church Street, Barnsley, South Yorkshire, S70 2AS, England
E-mail: enquiries@pen-and-sword.co.uk
Website: www.pen-and-sword.co.uk

or

PEN AND SWORD BOOKS
1950 Lawrence Rd, Havertown, PA 19083, USA
E-mail: Uspen-and-sword@casematepublishers.com
Website: www.penandswordbooks.com

Contents

Introduction

Whatever has led you to picking this book up, it's probably because you know that you're not right in the head and are ready to find out why.

This book will not only tell you why, but explain that this is completely normal in a world where normal doesn't really exist. Your normal and mine are likely to be very different, which is why people using the word are likely to confuse you, as you confuse others with your own definition.

Normal to an athlete is keeping their body in good shape and exercising regularly. This is not normal for your average resident at an elderly care home. For them normal is struggling with just about everything in their lives, and hopefully getting to the toilet in time. Normal for the average infant is wanting to have fun and screaming out when they want something, whereas normal for the average adult involves compromise on a regular basis.

At the time of writing, this manuscript had been sitting in my stored files for over seven years doing not very much. Then a friend who had read it had a random conversation with a publisher and here I am having to re-read it and write this during the biggest global pandemic in world history. The Coronavirus has given me time at home to sit back and watch the lunacy of the world unfold. I have always felt we lived in a lunatic asylum so the timing is incredible, tragic, and comical all at once.

In my original version it was a book on heart health; I then changed the title to *The Lunatic Gene*.

However, I was convinced that it needed to be about a self-destruct button, so here it is. It seems somehow more fitting right now as I witness stores being cleared of toilet rolls, world leaders clearly without a clue what's going on and social media creating a melting pot for bigotry, lunacy and stress.

Arguments over whether we should or shouldn't wear masks are breaking out everywhere, but I have witnessed most people wearing invisible masks for years. This is apparent now as true colours shine forth on social media and the news descends into the ridiculous. The effort of being right all of the time is overwhelming for many, even when they have no idea what's really going on. I certainly don't.

Masks are worn in life, business and at home. The concern is that if you were to reveal who you really are, warts and all, then people may not love you, or even like you on social media. The constant need for validation can become all-consuming and will eventually lead many to self-destruction. So now seems as good a time as any to be working on this again.

Even starting to attempt to make sense of the world that we live in through the lens of logic is a pointless task. We are emotional, energetic beings in a physical body. If you don't understand how your body, mind, thoughts and energy all interconnect, it is likely you will reach self-destruction sooner than most.

My confession.

At the time of writing this introduction I have just witnessed the death of my dad, heard that my friend and spiritual mentor died at the age of 38 in a fire and almost lost a few other good friends to Covid. In reading back through this manuscript I have realised that it is possible to know something without actually owning it, so this process has been profound in many ways.

So here I am, seven years after writing it, reading through it and realising that there is a lot of great advice and exercises in this book that I had stopped doing somewhere along the way. Nursing my dad at home for the past six years can do that, as can a growing sense of apathy and delusion. None of us are perfect!

It's more than just a little surreal reading a self-help book written by me to own my own lessons. Knowing something without owning it is pointless. In fact, it's worse than not knowing at all. However, I've re-read it and changed the introduction and first chapter for people like me who had stopped finding the time to read long books with drawn out content.

I'm not a guru, expert of new age spiritual teacher. I'm just someone with a lot of experience of working with those who have hit their own self-destruct button, often manifesting into serious physical and mental illness. Keeping a sense of humour has been an essential part of the journey. My personal manual for life came largely from watching *Monty Python* while growing up. The lessons in that have been surprisingly consistent as a guide for coping with life when it ventured into the not so fun zone.

I've certainly been on the brink of self-destruct a few times and the only reason that I am still here to write this is because of the support of some wonderful mentors and friends along the way. I've been there myself, and helped a few thousand people to accept pain, suffering and impending death in my roles as a nurse, counsellor and friend.

A different perspective.

Since as long as I can remember I have seen the world through a different lens, growing up in the grounds of a psychiatric hospital where my parents both worked as nurses. Normal for me was witnessing patients in night dresses and pyjamas knocking on our front door looking for cigarettes, and playing in the grounds where patients roamed around, curiously studying them from a distance. This was normal for me.

In the psychiatric hospital if anyone demonstrated any sort of desire to harm themselves or others they were drugged, locked up or electrocuted. Sometimes all three. This was normal in the '70s and '80s when I was there. So if you are looking for normal, you are probably barking up the wrong tree here. This is definitely not normal. I have been telling my friends for many years that the world outside of a lunatic asylum is a lot more dangerous and lunatic than anything inside it.

Have you been feeling guilty about your lack of will power or motivation to change your life and health in a positive way?

Maybe you have been telling yourself you need to be fitter or healthier, whilst indulging in occasional alcoholic beverages, smoking, or eating cakes and other sugary delights. If you have been told to give anything up and not yet done so, then you could be experiencing some inner conflict or guilt. This can cause your life to appear less than perfect at times and can lead to apathy, low mood, low confidence, sleeplessness, and stress.

With health experts all over the world telling you how easy it can be to look better, feel younger and give up everything you currently enjoy, it is easy to lose faith at times. At this stage you may be excused for feeling contempt towards these 'too good to be true' experts, or even lose the will to live.

One day you will indeed be dead. This is the only guarantee life gives you. You are unlikely to know when this day will come in advance; it could be decades down the line, or it may be today. Life can be notoriously unpredictable so you may as well accept you are not perfect and allow yourself a bit more flexibility at times. This book will help you with that.

Finding the middle ground.

During my time as a nurse in the National Health Service (NHS) I became known for my skills in dealing with patients nobody else could deal with. These *problem patients* had usually reached their breaking point and it was my job to work out what was wrong and do something about it. To do this I needed to form a new attitude different from the standard medical approach.

One day I met a man who had use of only 5% of his lung capacity. He was almost permanently attached to an oxygen mask and his quality of life was very poor. He suffered with Chronic Obstructive Pulmonary Disease (COPD), a progressively degenerative lung condition. His name was Alan.

I arrived to find the nurse from the previous shift in tears because Alan had been so rude to her. As she handed him over, there was no shortage of other nurses condemning Alan for being not only rude but stupid as well. He hadn't missed an opportunity all day to abuse the staff, cursing at them every time they walked past. It appeared I could be in for a challenging shift. I decided after handover that day to walk straight up to Alan and introduce myself to him.

He was furious.

After a suitably colourful array of expletives, he explained that all he wanted to do was smoke a cigarette. Because he had COPD, which had become worse during his admission, there was no way any of the staff were going to allow him to smoke. It was surely madness to do so?

I did not see it that way. Alan was not going to get any better through not smoking, and his stress level was off the scale at being told he could not smoke by nurses and doctors who often smelled of cigarettes. I brought him a wheelchair and told him to bring his cigarettes. I then wheeled him next to a window in the corridor where I could keep an eye on him whilst getting on with my daily tasks. A few minutes later I went to collect a smiling, happier man who had a reduced pulse, significantly lower blood pressure and a total personality overhaul.

The other staff were too busy to witness my intervention. They did, however, get to see a radically transformed Alan, who was now my new best friend. He was now not missing an opportunity to shower me with praise, to the surprise of the other staff. This was the day I realised preaching does not always work and seemingly bad habits can sometimes have a good outcome. The continuous stress of being told what not to do can be more damaging than doing it and accepting you are less than perfect.

Is your life giving you what you want?

Do you even know? I worked with the terminally ill for over a decade and can say for sure that it is likely you will experience a rapid change of focus when you face imminent death, unless you are prepared. If that day were to be today and you can honestly say you have done as much as you wanted to with your life in the time you've had, it is likely you do not need to read this book.

If, however, you feel frustrated, despondent, overwhelmed and in a sea of uncertainty then it is likely you are on the wrong path and missing the point of life, if there is any point at all. If guilt about your lifestyle is a daily companion for you then this book can help you to accept yourself and have a happier life.

I am not here to preach, advise or even influence you. I will ask you to question everything, not just in this book but in your entire life. My opinions have changed over time and may well change after writing this. My opinion is often controversial and I have had many interesting debates which have influenced me along my path. I aim only to share my journey with you up until this point and possibly give you a break from the waves of health experts telling you to give up the things you may currently like to do. If the threats of early death are getting tiresome for you then this book aims to offer you some hope and light relief.

Your heart has a separate intelligence from your head, and emotion is your guide.

When you allow your head to rule your heart, all sorts of undesirable manifestations can enter your life. These include doubt, pain, hurt, guilt, apathy and confusion. My journey has seen me let my head rule my heart for way too long at times, and has taken me to the precipice of death on more than a few occasions. As a nurse, witnessing friends and colleagues die early was very painful. Some took their own lives because they didn't ask for help.

Your heart is in constant communication with your head. That's the purpose of emotion. It is not positive or negative, it simply feels what your head is thinking. Thoughts and people that are toxic feel bad. When you are on the right track it feels good. If you are not feeling happy, energised and motivated then your emotion is letting you know your head does not yet get its message. If this status quo continues then your heart may well attack you. Since heart attacks are currently the biggest killer on the planet and mental illness is everywhere, it may be an idea to start understanding why. This book can show you how to think yourself to a better place.

How much is your wellbeing worth?

I have spoken to thousands of people who spent the healthiest years of their lives compromising their health to increase their wealth. Then, just after they retired, they had a health crisis and realised their money was suddenly less important than their health.

Millions, if not billions of people, realise too late their mental health is worth investing in. How much are you investing in your wellbeing right now?

One step at a time.

Only use what you feel works for you. You may do this in a linear way or just ask a question and flick the book open at a random page. Both ways work. My interviews with thousands of people who have experienced serious health issues, and my own personal experience, have contributed to my findings. Through asking searching questions the same patterns have emerged. These lifestyle and mindset factors often start years before serious physical and mental health issues manifest. Most doctors simply do not have time to go as deep into the issues as I did when I worked as a nurse.

Trust your first answers and instincts – this is what your heart wants you to act upon.

This process may bring up some surprising insights for you. You probably already know what you need to do to feel better; you just need a reminder and the confidence to do it. For this reason I encourage you to trust the first answers that come into your head when you think about the questions in this book, and maybe use a journal. If your answer makes no sense to you then this is almost certainly from the part of your mind that you had stopped trusting. Use it, feel it, trust it.

This is not a logical journey.

You are an emotional being. At the centre of all emotion is your heart. Using your head to analyse this is the reason why you get ill or feel bad. It is what you feel that really matters on this voyage of discovery. Thinking without feeling is the reason so many people never realise what is truly important. So many people develop unconscious ways to detach from their emotions, leading to not so nice feelings. For this reason I encourage you to feel what is right for you and question everything in this book and in your life.

If you read something that causes a reaction in your body, especially in your heart, then pay careful attention. The words in this book are for your heart, straight from mine. What your head thinks about it is of secondary concern. If you could solve your own lunacy with your head, you wouldn't be reading this. Start now by tuning into your body and noticing what's going on. Your happiness depends on your ability to align your thoughts with your emotions and stop making your thoughts lead you to places that feel bad.

Your voyage of discovery is about to begin.

If you are short of time then chapter one will give you enough to know what you need to do. If you are ready to own it there are exercises at the end of each chapter to help you. Or you may just choose to skip through them for now and go back to them when you actually hit a brick wall and feel that therapy is not an option you are ready for. I also tried to work through my self-destruct issues on my own a few times, which is an almost impossible task. Especially for the average adult. So I wish you good luck on your quest to feel better by understanding the signs and symptoms of what can lead you to self-destruct, and offer you a few ways to identify the early warning signs and avert it.

Chapter 1

The Root of All Self-Destruction in Four Words

Your relationship with yourself.

I could almost stop writing right now, but my publishing contract tells me I need more, so the rest of the book will elaborate on this point, and this chapter is for you once you've read the book once and just need a recap. The rest of it is just a guide to how to improve your own relationship with yourself. This is the only way to avoid self-destruct. The moment you stopped prioritising this was the moment that your mental health started venturing in the wrong direction.

We can identify hundreds, if not thousands, of facets of what leads to self-destruction, yet they all stem from a single place: your relationship with yourself. If you don't have a loving relationship with yourself, which is most of the planet right now, then you are already on the route to self-destruction. In fact, if you want to know the root cause of every problem in your universe, there it is. Every single other problem in your world is a direct result of a poor relationship with yourself.

The solution: learn to love yourself more.

If you are like me, you like to get to the point quickly, so I've taken the liberty of doing that for you. Everybody will press their self-destruct button during their life, usually several times. It happens when we hit a point of feeling powerless and trapped in our own thoughts, usually underpinned by the opinions and beliefs of others.

This is the simple truth. Feeling lost, angry, sad, desolate, empty and guilty is all part of the journey. If you didn't feel not so good you would end up living someone else's life. It is often necessary to get angry to motivate positive change. To do that you will need to acknowledge that nobody knows what is best for you better than you do. Whatever opinions, advice and limitations that well-meaning friends and family members tell you, if they don't feel good, they probably are wrong for you.

Your emotions are your guide to happiness.

The difference between those who have a peaceful death and those who suffer greatly at the end usually comes down to one simple equation; how happy are you with your life? If you are not happy now then something needs to change. In virtually every case of someone with advanced mental and medical illness there are a host of frequent fliers that indicate the major factors that cause this, all of them stemming from a lack of self-love, belief and hope.

Being trapped in a job or relationship are two of the key players in the slow descent towards self-destruct. Bullying bosses, work colleagues or spouses are key players in this equation, along with beliefs that you cannot afford to leave them. I have heard this gem from so many people I've worked with who had strokes, heart attacks or cancer. Your body will eventually respond to constant negative thoughts and feelings by giving you a way out of that feeling of being trapped – by killing you early. It's so important to know this as it's one of the main causes of physical and mental illness that I hear.

The root of all unhappiness.

The only way to live a happy life is to lose judgement. Judgement is the parent of blame.

There is no question that some of the actions of others are less than ethical. However, only by taking responsibility for your own actions will you ever find a happier path. I have listened to many patients, clients and friends consistently blame someone else for all their problems. Blame is very convenient as it often divorces us from the cause of our problems. I have done this enough in the past to not judge anyone else for the situations that they find themselves in.

It's easy to feel disempowered when certain people and situations seem necessary for survival. From sharing a house with a partner who provides for you financially but undermines your confidence, to listening to the bullying boss who brings all their personal problems to work and takes them out on you. This is a toxic zone that can seem hopeless when your confidence has been eroded.

At the other side of the spectrum is having achieved everything that you thought was important and wondering what else there is to truly live for.

Finding some sort of purpose with life is something that everyone searches for at some stage, provided that they live long enough.

From judgement comes guilt.

Guilt is the direct result of blaming others for aspects of ourselves. This is the doctor or nurse who tells someone to give up drinking and smoking and then goes to the pub to do it themselves. Or the parent who tells their children not to do the things that they themselves do regularly. Such hypocrisy can create all sorts of problems. This wellbeing paradox causes judgement and guilt. Interestingly, in the Tibetan language there is no translation for guilt. The closest translation is intelligent regret that decides to do things differently.

How useful would it be if everyone started using that version of guilt?

Unfortunately, judgement leads to guilt, which leads to more judgement, which leads to mental and physical illness for so many people I have spoken to. This is more than unfortunate and is the inevitable cycle responsible for most physical and mental illnesses.

Expectations of others is a key player here.

I have met enough narcissists and sociopaths in relationships to know that they will not know or care that you are getting ill because of their actions, because they are not able to experience empathy. They can present well and make you feel great, before ripping strips off your confidence slowly for as long as you let them. The slow decline is usually subtle and then one day you may wake up with no confidence or motivation to do anything and an overwhelming sense of doom.

In these cases it's often necessary to feel anger in order to find the courage to do what's needed to be done. However, everyone is attracted into your life for a reason. It is your struggle that makes you who you are. And ultimately, you can only follow a better path when you value your own happiness enough to take the necessary action to want something better and take action towards it. I certainly put others before myself for much of my life and needed several wake-up calls to break free of this hold and put my own happiness as a priority.

There is no such thing as a negative emotion.

All emotion is a guide. Some emotions may feel negative, but they have a positive intention. It's perfectly normal to feel sad, angry, frustrated and hurt. These are simply your heart's guide to things that need to change. Feeling sad after the loss of a loved one is a reasonable emotion. It isn't negative, it just shows that you care and makes you more human. However, if you are feeling sad and hurt for more than a few months about the same thing without taking action to resolve it, then it's definitely a guide for change.

This change begins by asking yourself; what would make me feel happier? The crucial element of this is that if you make your happiness dependent on anyone else you are giving away your power. So many problems are caused by believing that others must change in order to ensure your happiness. This is disempowerment and born from a lack of self-love.

Your ability to prioritise your happiness independently of what others think or do is the key to your own physical and mental wellbeing. Expecting others to change to facilitate this is not a sustainable solution, and the key to most marriage challenges. If the compromise is one-sided against you then it's your job to amend your own behaviour, regardless of how difficult that may seem at the moment. Your emotions are your guide.

Know what makes you happy.

If you are unhappy it's your job to work out how you can make yourself happier. If the people who tell you that they love you do not want to facilitate this, then it's not true love. In my world true love is being able to let someone go if they are unhappy in a relationship.

If it is real love you will continue to love that person and they will continue to love you regardless of what you are both doing with your lives. But this comes with a big disclaimer as I have never married and will never claim to be a relationship expert! I did witness the heartbreak of my dad's partner of 20 years asking him to leave when she knew she had dementia. He didn't and told nobody about it. One day the stress of not being able to leave his flat because he would be locked out of it led him to a stroke. They both needed care after this. It was truly heartbreaking to see.

Such selfless acts of love I would witness all the time as a nurse. I also witnessed couples who had been together for 30 plus years die within days or weeks of each other. My grandparents were married for 68 years. The night before my grandad died we were told that he had the rest of the ward in stitches laughing. He went to sleep and never woke up. The next day my granny had a heart attack and died a few weeks later. They were 94 and 90, respectively. This is very common.

You may get caught in two minds.

If you have used this expression before then you know the feeling of receiving contradictory information internally. You have two minds: your conscious and your unconscious mind. They work a little bit like thunder and lightning.

Your unconscious mind works quickly and gives you information from a higher source. It is there to serve you on a higher plane, is bright but often not heard. Some call it a gut instinct or intuition. It is like lightning and comes quickly and can go just as fast for some people.

Your conscious mind is slower and louder and, like thunder, makes a lot of noise and will cause you to take more notice. This can be other people's agendas and programming entering your mind. Listening to this all the time can lead to you not hearing what your heart wants you to know.

Intuition and gut instinct are your guides to happiness.

A great example of this is when you see a quiz and you get drawn to a certain answer, but you don't know where from. You may then talk yourself out of it, only to find out it was right. Tuning into your intuition is a big part of finding your happiness.

You are made of energy.

Your thoughts, your deeds, your body and your mind are all energetic. If you are unfamiliar to the worlds of energy and intuition, we will be visiting this throughout the book. As a starter: have you ever thought of someone and then they have contacted you? This is because your thoughts are energy.

We've covered a few things in this chapter so now we will look at small steps that you can take in a better direction in the next.

Exercise: What is the one thing in your life that if you changed would make you feel the happiest? You can find this out by thinking about the outcome and noticing how it feels.

Chapter 2

Small Things Can Make a Big Difference

When your self-destruct button activates, it's often from a place of overwhelm.

If you have activated your self-destruct button the odds are that there have been hundreds, if not thousands, of small steps in the wrong direction, which is why it can all appear as so overwhelming. The thought of getting out of the situation that you find yourself in is often too much to bear, which is probably why the self-destruct button was activated in the first place.

Often this is amplified by a poor state of health. Symptoms that things are going wrong can include insomnia, weight/appetite problems, hypertension, headaches on a more frequent basis, irritability, anger, depression – and that's just a few of them. We will look at some of the others later.

Quite often people prioritise money over health.

This can manifest negatively if you find yourself in a job that you hate or even in multiple jobs to pay the accumulating bills that you have. Necessity creates misery in this instance and it only leads to one place: misery. Before you know it your energy and motivation to spend any time focussing on your health and wellbeing becomes a distant memory, and the decline starts.

The paradox of focusing on money, when health is essential to being able to enjoy it, is tragic. In life, I have noticed the human potential for taking the wonderful things and people in their lives for granted and focusing more on what is missing. We are goal-orientated animals, constantly striving for something better. My numerous conversations with my patients during my nursing years have yielded a very common theme.

When you are young, it is usual for your health to be high and your money to be low. Consequently, you are far more likely to focus on what you don't have – in this case, money. Throughout life it makes sense to you that the more money you have, the better life will be if you ever reach retirement age (and possibly for you, the thought of not living to retirement age is just something that happens to other people).

Many people spend years, sometimes decades, in unfulfilling jobs or relationships they are not happy with, thus compromising their mental health. The fear of the financial ramifications of leaving a well-paid but utterly frustrating job or a loveless relationship results in extreme compromise. This can be detrimental to your health. Consequently, as time progresses, your money increases and your health decreases. Most people do not even notice as the crossover happens.

The point of no return.

This happens one day when you experience a health crisis. For many people this is around their retirement. Just when they were so close to living the retirement dream, they end up in a hospital bed with the news their health is irreversibly bad. Having sat down with hundreds of people who have found themselves in this position, I know what this looks and sounds like. Devastation is somehow not a strong enough term to describe how this place feels. From here, there is plenty of time to reflect on how people wished their health was better.

Often when this happens, people would gladly pay as much as they could afford to get their health back. Unfortunately, it's too late. Whilst almost all of those I spoke to had spent their whole lives investing small amounts regularly in a pension, they invested almost nothing in their health.

The Dalai Lama summarises it well:

When asked what surprises him most about humanity, he replied:

'Man.

Because he sacrifices his health in order to make money.

Then he sacrifices his money to recuperate his health.

And then he is so anxious about the future that he does not enjoy the present.

The result being that he does not live either in the present or the future.

He lives as if he is never going to die.

And then dies having never really lived.'

This quote encapsulates what I witnessed as a nurse. If only more people moved through life constantly balancing the future of their health with the future of their finances, we would live on a happier planet. Having looked after as many sick people as I have, I can assure you when serious illness strikes, regardless of what you have in your bank account, money will be of little consolation to you.

This is not to say money is not important: it is. But it has to be balanced with good health if you want to enjoy it for longer when you have it. Good health is not merely the absence of disease, which many people consider it to be, it is something needing to be consistently addressed, maintained and invested in. I cannot emphasise this point enough.

The simple things are often the most important.

One of my roles as a nurse was to measure the fluid balance of certain patients. This was particularly important for anyone who had presented with heart failure. This condition, as its name probably suggests to you, happens when a heart gets old and tired. Consequently, it is not as efficient and excess fluid can build up around the body. This often presents with excessive amounts of fluid around people's legs. This is a condition called oedema. People with heart failure were usually on a restricted fluid intake, in order to reduce the swelling in their legs. People with urinary infections would also be put on a fluid balance chart, along with elderly, clearly malnourished, patients.

I found that over 95% of the patients I assessed and conducted fluid balance charts on had spent most of their lives dehydrated. We had been told that any caffeinated drink should not be counted towards fluid intake, as caffeine is a diuretic. But time after time, I noticed that many people drank nothing but caffeine. Interestingly enough, there were about 5–6 coffee rounds a day in the hospitals where I worked. This was one of many ironies of the health system I witnessed. The good news is your body is highly adaptable and can tolerate such changes for long periods. The bad news is it will always catch up with you eventually.

Dehydration takes its toll.

Let us look at a few facts about dehydration:

- Fluid loss of more than 1% of body weight can lead to reduction in performance and inability to control body temperature.

- Dehydration of 4% or more can lead to more severe loss of performance as well as difficulties in concentration, headaches, irritability, sleepiness and increased respiration rates and body temperature.
- Dehydration of 10% or more of your body weight can be fatal.

Dehydration often manifests as hunger (a great weight-loss strategy is to drink a pint of water whenever you feel hungry in between meals). It can also affect your mood, short-term memory, and alertness.

Such a simple thing so few people fully understand. Being properly hydrated is the answer to so many of the weight, diet, health and performance issues people tend to struggle with. Add that around 75% of the brain is made up of water and you can directly equate dehydration to some headaches and almost all poor performance at work and in life.

Red Hot Tip: Take a glass of water to bed with you and drink it as soon as you wake up. If you want to take it to another level write, 'I love you' and stick it to the glass or place it underneath it overnight.

A swift word of caution before you decide this is your 'Eureka!' moment and spend your whole day drinking water and nothing else; you need to balance your electrolytes. Your body must have a balance of sugar and salt with all fluids you take.

Since your body is continually producing waste products, it makes sense to start your day with a glass of water. In the same way not flushing a toilet would become unpleasant over time, your body needs water to flush out the wastage. You can tell the degree of dehydration you have by observing the colour of your urine. The darker and more concentrated it is, the more dehydration you have. I realise this is a really nursing thing to say and it is easier for men to do than for women but every opportunity to help you to know your body better – I'll take it.

The good news is I will not start suggesting you start rummaging through your used toilet bowl to find what fascinating things are coming out of your body – there are other people who will do this for you. Observing and recording the details of patients' faeces was one of the less pleasant aspects of my life as a nurse.

My personal life hack is to balance every not so good habit with a good one. I love coffee so if I'm having a cup of coffee in the morning I precede it with a glass of water of at least the same size. This way every not so good habit is the trigger for something good.

Learn how to ground yourself.

Any electrician knows if you do not ground an electrical current then it can become unsafe. Most non-electricians also appreciate this fact. Your heart emits an electrical current which can be measured anywhere else in your body. If you have ever had an Electrocardiogram (ECG) then you know what I mean.

It is just as important for you to be able to ground the energy of your heart in order to maintain your own safety. Just in case you are wondering why you need to learn how to ground your energy regularly, we will take a look at some of the symptoms of not being grounded:

- Inability to focus on one task (easily distracted)
- Lower motivation and/or energy
- Feeling the need for extra caffeine to get you through the day
- Tiredness
- Irritability
- Feeling like you do not belong
- Detachment from responsibility
- Inability to explain yourself in a way that those around you understand
- In extreme cases, depression and suicidal thoughts

How do you ground yourself?

In order to ground it is not necessary to be able to see, hear, feel or even believe it is working. Because your energy follows your thoughts, it is only necessary to think about it. You may well see or feel something during this process but it is not important whether you do or not.

As you do this exercise, you may wish to close your eyes. When you do, just imagine there is a big ball of energy in the centre of the Earth and think about a cord coming from it and connecting to the base of your spine. You are now grounded. When you are grounded you allow the energy of the Earth to enter your body, which can allow you to feel more connected. It also helps to remove certain energy from your body that is not serving you. This exercise can be done in under a second when you are used to it and it will improve your focus and motivation throughout the day.

If you are not yet familiar with the world of energy medicine and how it works, that's OK. Just notice the soles of your feet and feel them connect with the ground in whatever way works for you. Just thinking about your feet and the ground will ground you. There are hundreds of ways to do this and whatever works for you, go with it.

You have two choices with grounding.

If you are experiencing the same feelings as I when first told about grounding, you may not exactly be convinced it will work for you. Indeed, I spent years working with energy, not remembering to ground my energy and wondering why so many strange things were happening to me. The idea that grounding worked, when it was so simple to do, did not resonate with my medically-trained, nursing mind.

Grounding really does work but I don't want you to take my word for it, I want you to do it and decide for yourself. Since it can be done almost instantly then it would be a shame to not at least experiment with this for a while.

You can be like me for the first few years after my training and not believe it or do it. Alternatively, you can identify the list of symptoms of not being grounded I listed just now, be open-minded, give it a go and find out for yourself. From this point you can just do the exercise regularly and see if it improves your energy, focus, motivation, health, happiness and life. If it works for you, use it. If not, don't.

How to control your mood.

There will be times when life deals you a testing situation, which may bring up more emotion for you than normal. It is times like this you will need all the help you can get. The technique I am about to show you is as close as I can give you to a magic wand for your mood.

Your body needs oxygen. Your heart is constantly beating so blood can get to your lungs, where it picks up oxygen and transports it to the rest of your body. This process is dependent on there being a constantly renewed source of oxygen in your lungs. Your breathing is responsible for this.

One of the skills we learned as nurses was how to observe a patient's breathing rate. A recommended healthy breathing rate for the average adult is about 7 breaths per minute when they are at rest. This allows you to properly empty your lungs of the waste products and properly fill them with a fresh supply of oxygen. The average respiration rate of patients in a hospital ward is about 20 breaths per minute. This doesn't include those with acute asthma or other chronic and acute breathing conditions.

At this rate, your lungs never get properly filled or properly emptied. Because of this, there are more waste products in your lungs and less oxygen at any given moment. This means your heart has to work harder to get the amount of oxygen your body needs. The equivalent analogy would be keeping an outdoor swimming pool untreated over the winter. In the Summer, when it is filled with dirt, insects and leaves, your cleaning solution would involve cleaning out about 10% of the dirty water and filling it up with clean water. The dirt at the bottom of the pool would remain in place. This cycle would be repeated every time you thought it needed cleaning.

Clearly, your pool would never be clean and your desire to swim in it would be somewhat diminished. Yet, this is how most people treat their lungs for most of their lives. This puts more stress on your heart, which could be easily avoided.

Your breathing controls your mood.

If you meditate or do an exercise like Tai Chi, Yoga or Chi Gung then you already know this simple truth. If you do not yet then it's time to learn how to breathe properly. When you inhale, do it from your belly, filling it completely before you allow your chest to fill as well. Because your lungs are much bigger than most people realise, it is important to know what it feels like to breathe properly. Keep breathing in, until you cannot any more, hold it for a few seconds and then breathe out very slowly. Ensure you have exhaled as much breath as you can. Repeat this as many times as you feel inclined to.

It is likely, if you have done this exercise properly, you started to feel light-headed after just a few breaths. This is because you are not used to breathing properly very often, and breathing correctly can slow your heart rate down, instantly reducing stress. Your heart rate can slow down because there is more oxygen in your lungs and less work for your blood and heart to do. If you want to take this to a whole new level I suggest you look up the Wim Hof Method.

During my time living in Thailand, I took myself off to a silent meditation retreat on four separate occasions. Only through having this lesson drilled into me consistently, was I able to get a really deep understanding of the power slowing down your breathing can bring. After ten days of silent meditation, I was able to breathe less than one breath per minute during some meditations. I spent one meditation counting my breaths. It was a 30 min meditation and I counted 23 breaths. It was the first ever meditation that I did not want to end, even if it did take an extreme situation to get me there. It is very easy to relax when your breathing gets deeper. Learning to do this regularly in the busy, western world is not so easy.

I have found this since returning to the UK. It is all too easy to not prioritise a time-out to just breathe uninterrupted, so start with just a minute or two and work your way up. This is an easier way for most people to start. It's also possible to do this when walking.

Exercise: Each morning for the next week (longer if you want even better results), start your day with a glass of water, five deep breaths and grounding yourself. Write a reminder and put it where you will see it every morning. Somewhere in your bedroom is an excellent place. If you feel even more adventurous then add an entry to your journal explaining how you feel and whether there is any noticeable difference.

With your breathing deeper and mood more relaxed, you will now be perfectly set up to give yourself a health check and cut any ties no longer serving you, which we shall discuss in the next chapter.

Chapter 3

How to Cut The Ties Holding You Back

I have never really been one for superstition, which is why I defiantly chose 13 as my lucky number from a young age. The fact 13 has been branded as unlucky by many made me feel there would be plenty of luck needed to balance out all of the bad luck that others drew from it. As a boy, my granny would refuse to cross me on the stairs and stopped me from walking under ladders because she deemed it unlucky. Superstition is a funny thing. The well researched Maharishi Effect has demonstrated that if enough people believe something then it may well have an influence on other people. Reading this chapter could be very lucky for you!

It's time for you to start influencing.

You may well be the best negotiator in the world, with a glowing track record. If you are, well done. If you are not then you are about to fine-tune your skills. You are going to learn how to influence your body in this section. In order to do this we are going to move your attention away from your external world and towards your internal world.

So many people spend almost all of their lives focusing their attention, energy and influencing potential on the things happening outside of their bodies. Because you now know energy follows thought and are open to the possibility your thoughts have the power to heal your body, then it makes sense to learn how to energise your body.

How to energise your body.

There are no set rules for this process. Indeed, any energetic process involving your thoughts is only restricted by your imagination. I encourage you to find your own way with this exercise and go with what feels right for you.

Get yourself in a comfortable position, ground yourself and focus on making your breathing deeper. Do this for at least a minute. Notice how you feel. Intend to communicate with your heart and body during this process, paying particular attention to how you feel.

When you feel completely relaxed, imagine bright white light entering your body through your head and from your grounding cord, and filling up inside you and in the area surrounding you. When you have done this, you can give yourself a body scan. There are no rules or expectations here. All you need to do is focus your attention on the tips of your toes and slowly move your attention up your body, noticing if you can feel any aches, pains or blockages. As you do, imagine white light entering your body to relax, restore and energise yourself.

Once you have scanned your whole body, you can focus your attention on any areas where there were aches, pains or blockages. As you do, ask 'What do you need me to know in order to release you?' As you do this pay close attention to any insights you get and constantly focus on making your breathing deeper. It is important you not only get the message(s) but also act accordingly. The longer you spend doing this, the better you will feel. Whilst your aches and pains may not miraculously vanish straight away, this exercise will always benefit you, even if it is just at a subtle level. Your body is in constant communication with your heart and mind. This is your opportunity to listen to what it wants you to know.

Another exercise to energise your heart is to put all of your attention inside your heart and ask: 'What do you want me to know?' As you do this, imagine bright light filling up your heart and energising every drop of blood passing through it. Intend for your new, energised blood to pass through your arteries and veins, relaxing them and dissolving any fatty deposits it comes across. Repeat this for as long as you like, as often as you like.

Perform a phone health check.

Everyone in your life influences your energy and health just by you thinking about them. The thought of some people will cause you to feel better, think healthy, energising thoughts and cheer up your day. Other people will cause your energy to drop, throw you out of your flow, or trigger your fight or flight response. In order for this to happen, you only have to be reminded of the people in question.

Whenever I talk to my clients about the contacts on their phone, I give them what I call a Phone-Shui. I go through their contacts and ask them to give a rating between one to ten of how happy they would feel if that person phoned right now. I go through this process for each person on their phone contact list. I have yet to find someone who has come to me with a major problem and a phone full of contacts all above five. Often, there are a few people who are a one or two and cause them to feel instantly worse. I watch people's energy drain instantly as I read out the names.

I frequently find ex-boyfriends/girlfriends who have not been fully dealt with and have bad associations. Some have friends of many years, who always dump on them, going from one problem to another. Some have family members, who are always quick to criticise and help facilitate feelings of anger, frustration, guilt or inadequacy.

Ask yourself: what is the benefit to you of having someone on your phone who consistently helps you to feel bad?

When I perform this exercise I usually get blank, confused looks as though my clients had no control over the contacts they kept on their phone. So many ridiculous excuses are presented to me as to why certain people remain on their phones. I should know; I had been making them unconsciously for over a decade because nobody had ever challenged me on this. Things like, 'But I've known them for years' or 'I need to keep their number so I know who it is if they call.'

For whatever reason you feel five or less about any of your phone contacts, there is no good reason, from your heart's perspective, to keep them on your phone. If you are feeling incredibly connected, happy with your life, have plenty of time to spare and enjoy listening to people's problems repeatedly, then by all means, keep who ever you like on your phone. If not, then it's time to delete.

Real friends are honest with each other.

If you have any friends, and I use this word in its broadest context, on your phone who cause a knot in your stomach when you see their name come up as they call you, then your heart is speaking to you. It is common to feel friends of many years deserve unquestioning loyalty. Even when their life path has taken them to a place where they complain all the time, do not listen to helpful advice, and drain the energy of whoever is unfortunate enough to listen to them. Some people do not want you to solve their problem(s), even though they say they do, which we will discuss later on. If you find yourself in this situation then you are not being a good friend by maintaining this status quo.

Sometimes it is necessary to stop playing the good cop and be the bad cop.

When I first had the realisation that I did not have the time, energy or resources to prop up some very good friends from my past who had found themselves in dark places seemingly all the time, I knew things had to change. I had known one of my phone contacts at the time for about 15 years. We had been through many good times and he had been great when I had a very challenging problem 13 years earlier. However, our friendship had become increasingly one-way traffic. At least 95% of all our conversations were about his problems. I would offer advice, which was rarely taken, and the cycle continued.

I eventually reached a place where I needed to look after me more. I no longer had the time or energy to listen to the same issues repeatedly, even though this was one of my longest friendships. Loyalty is an admirable quality and a value I hold very highly. However, I had reached my breaking point.

It took me to be financially and emotionally broken to be angry and ruthless enough to do what needed to be done.

To discover this lesson I had to let my personal heart health reach a very low point indeed. Coming from someone who liked to keep everyone happy, especially those who I called my friends, it was a particularly testing time. One by one, I deleted everyone from my phone who I would rather not talk to. It was uncomfortable at first but I felt great at the end of it.

Honesty is essential in any relationship.

Over the next months, I ran into a few of the people whose numbers I had deleted. Many of the exchanges were very similar. When accused of not phoning or being a stranger I informed each of them what I had done and how they had made me feel. Being honest is one of the most important aspects a friendship can have. Life has taught me that my really good friends are prepared to risk the friendship in order to give me a kick up the arse that I need.

They are doing it from a place of love and if the friendship is worthwhile I see this and bounce back, thanking them. I have seen this in a professional capacity as a nurse and now I had taken it into my circle of friends. Some made me feel good most of the time, and others would constantly drain my energy.

If your friends cannot be honest with you then who can be?

Reactions from being honest to such friends will usually go one of two ways. They will either take such offence at what you say and will not speak to you again, at least for a very long time. This situation is a win for you. Alternatively, they will get a wake up call, change their behaviour and thank you for facilitating this realisation. This is also a win for you and a bigger win for your friend.

After undergoing this process with everyone on my phone who was a five or less, my energy, motivation and focus all changed in a very positive way.

These days I refuse to keep anyone on my phone I consider to be less than a seven. You may wish to take it to this level if you feel so inclined but, for now, I urge you to seriously evaluate the effect YOUR CHOICES of people on your phone are currently having on the health of your heart and your entire state of wellbeing. If you delete certain numbers and do not recognise these people when they phone then let all unknown calls go to answer phone. You can always listen to the message and phone anyone important back straight away.

If you meet someone new and enter their number on your phone, start noting how you feel at the end of each call. If you get three or more scores of five or less: delete them.

It is highly likely you may not be comfortable performing this exercise.

This is OK. If you have spent a lifetime accumulating contacts on your phone, I would not expect you to instantly believe what I am saying in this section. You may not feel comfortable questioning every person in your life yet, as this can be a challenging experience. If this is you then please stay open-minded. This may seem like a less than comfortable experience but I want you to start valuing your time and your energy as the most important thing in your life. Would it be better spent doing something you love, with people who you love, or listening to the same, energy-draining ridiculousness of those who clearly have no concern for how you feel about listening to it?

The principle of energetic ties.

Everybody in your life right now is tied to you energetically. Because energy follows thought, their appearance on your phone helps keep them with you in your life, unconsciously, even when they are not.

Each of us only has room for a certain amount of energetic ties we give most of our energy or attention to. If you are spending a percentage of your time looking to be an emotional dumping ground for others then it will have two major ramifications in your life. Firstly, you will not have as much time or energy to attract new, positive people into your life who can help you to feel better. Secondly, it will have a negative impact on your energy, which your other friends will need to compensate for. This could even affect them to the point that your more positive friends want to spend less time with you because you are complaining more.

If someone has had a bad day and decides to tell you all about it in glorious detail, explaining every cruel twist of fate that has adversely challenged them, then unless you are trained in advanced energy clearing and restoration techniques, you will feel worse after listening to them. Just suppose your best and most positive friend was to phone you straight after hearing this and ask you how you were.

It is highly likely your thoughts would be filled with the issues that had just been dumped on you. When this happens it is likely you would offload some of this negative energy on your good friend, in order to help you cope. This would then have a negative impact on their energy. When people dump their problems on you, without giving back, they are handing you their energetic bin bags, full of crap. It is then your job to deal with them. Will you deal with them yourself or pass them on to another friend?

Energy principles for your body and friends are similar to the electricity in your house.

I am no electrician but I understand the basics of how electricity works in the average house. You have a main fuse box, which is connected to a central source and sockets all over your house. From these sockets, numerous electrical items can function simultaneously. Many of these items will work harmoniously and make your life easier. However, some appliances may not work, or even cause your entire system to short circuit. This is a necessary safety measure, caused by grounding the current.

Staying connected to the central source is essential, otherwise you will lose power or will need to connect with another supply. This is the equivalent of grounding your energy. Your body can feed off the energy supply of other people, which can work when you are not connected to the central source. When people get caught in cycles of negativity they have lost connection to the central source and need to hook into another supply. They will often use their story or problem to do this. This method is dependent on other people's willingness to supply them. This method can also cause problems for those to whom they connect to.

Within a house, each appliance is connected with a plug. Within your energy field the thoughts, incidents and people you focus on are the same as the appliances connected within your house. Each one needs the energy of your central supply. Your heart provides this energy. When you and the person who you are talking to are connected to the central supply, there will be a wonderful flow of energy, often creating electrical synergy.

You allow anything or anyone you think about to plug into your energy supply.

Some of these people and thoughts will energise you; others will drain you. When an appliance ceases to work in your house, or a person or thought in your energy field, there are two obvious options: fix it or replace it. If you intend to fix it then you will need to change something. If you leave it plugged in and not working, it will not serve you, and could stop you from using another, more useful appliance. Your energy field uses the same principle. If you are thinking about anything not working for you it can be pointless at best and damaging at worst. These people will definitely accelerate your path to your self-destruct button.

With electricity, if you touch a live current it causes your fingers to constrict. Testing an electric current with your hand is generally not a good idea. If, for whatever reason, you decide this is the only course of action, it pays to know touching it with the back of your hand will constrict your muscles away from it, if it is live. This causes a short, sharp shock. Maybe you have had a few of those in your life. If, however, you test an electrical current with the front of your hand, it can cause your fingers to move towards the current, giving you a bigger shock. This is what happens to your energy field when you focus on a problem, rather than a possible solution.

Sometimes an appliance will short-circuit your house and your connection to the central source will be cut. This can happen to your energy field when someone or something enters your life and does not have your best interests at the top of their agenda.

When you spend time continuously thinking about people or things which do not make you feel good, it can short-circuit your flow of energy. When this happens you need to reconnect to the central supply. A breakup in a relationship would be a perfect example of this. The news can often short-circuit your entire system, yet staying connected to it in your thoughts helps nobody. When this happens you will need to draw off other people's energy until you disconnect from the relationship and reconnect with the central supply. The central supply here is your grounding cord, powered by self-love.

Your energy supply, like the electrical supply in your house, will cause certain appliances to stop working over time. You may fix the appliance by changing the component that isn't working, or replace it. You can do this in your energy field by cutting energetic cords. By cutting the cords with all of the people, thoughts, and beliefs in your life no longer working for you, it clears space for new people, thoughts, and beliefs to replace them.

If you are anything less than enlightened then this process will impact your entire life. If you cannot clear and release other people's energy instantly I recommend you seriously review every name on your phone. This exercise has the ability to increase your heart health with immediate effect.

Exercise: Give yourself a health check. Ground yourself and scan your body, sending energy to any areas that may be painful, aching or blocked. Notice any insights or messages which come up for you during this process and act upon them. Then perform a phone health check, removing anyone who is five or less.

You may also wish to do the same exercise with your thoughts:

Exercise: Ground yourself, take some deep breaths and close your eyes if you feel drawn to do so. Imagine a huge stage in front of you. Invite all of the people in your life upon it and thank ALL of them for bringing you to the place you are at now and allowing you to learn. Now ask everyone who no longer serves you in this current moment to leave. When you have done this, set your intention towards who or what you are looking to attract.

Now you have done your health check, cut some ties and invited helpful and energising people into your life, it is time to take a more detailed look into the world of energy. We will look at how healing your parents as a child has impacted your entire life.

Chapter 4

A More Detailed Look at Energy

Everything is energy.

Your body, your mind, your thoughts, the planet and everything you have ever known are made up of energy. This is the conclusion of the famous equation by Albert Einstein: $E=MC^2$.

Your energetic field is magnetic and you are like an energetic magnet, drawing towards you things and people that resonate with something within you. Some of this is influenced through your thoughts, which you have the power to change at any given moment. The rest is influenced by unconscious programmes, which you have picked up along the way.

Your unconscious programming comes in two main forms: other people's beliefs and other people's energy, much of which you took on board when you were too young to remember. This is because your magnetic, energetic field is like a sponge for other people's energy and beliefs in the first few years of your life.

You healed your parents.

As a child, before you developed the ability to fight or flight, you had to adopt another strategy to deal with certain situations. Since you were a bundle of pure love and openness, you had no filters as to what was right, wrong, good or bad. Your parents were there to love you and nurture you. They held you and spoke gently to you. They fed you and soothed you.

However, one day they probably appeared angry, frustrated, sad or guilty to you. This would have been a shock and you would have wanted them to feel better so they could be loving again. All you knew was that something was different. Without thinking about it, you absorbed some of their negative energy. The result was your parents felt better and you felt slightly worse. As this process does not happen consciously you keep this energy until you learn to identify and release it. Often, this energy plays out, unidentified, for the rest of people's lives. This is because these things are not commonly taught or understood.

Did you ever criticise a parent for doing something and then do it yourself?

This trait is all too common. Because you healed your parents by taking on board their energy, it can replay, without you realising how or what caused it.

Something triggers the response and, before you realise it, you seem to have become your parent(s). This may only happen for brief moments before you snap out of it and wonder how you possibly managed to do or say what you just did. This is unconscious programming and it will continue to replay until you identify what triggers it.

This also happens with beliefs.

In your vulnerable, open state, your parents can tell you anything and you will believe it to be true. If your parents spent time telling you how beautiful, brilliant and wonderful you were all the time then the odds are you are not reading this book. If, however, your parents may have embedded a few less than empowering beliefs within you in between the niceties then it is like a hypnotic suggestion to you just waiting for something to trigger it. You can spend decades not realising you are filled with these unconscious triggers, which play out when they are activated.

Kim had spent years going from one unsuccessful relationship to another, accumulating an impressive list of men who simply abused her good, loving and caring nature. Her first serious boyfriend had left her the minute he found out she was pregnant and left her to bring up a child alone. Successive boyfriends had all left after just a few months, one taking a sizeable amount of money from her. She was desperate and almost broken. She had felt suicidal at times, only brought out of it by the thought of her little boy.

After a full day of intense therapy, Kim discovered she held a belief which shocked her: 'Men just cannot be trusted.' Her mum had repeated this, like a mantra to Kim, as her parents were divorced soon after her birth. Consequently, Kim grew up programmed to not trust men. Her magnetic energy field then repeatedly and unconsciously attracted men who fitted perfectly into this programme, which had been running unconsciously for most of her life. Consciously, Kim wanted to trust and love the men in her life but couldn't understand why she was so seemingly unlucky in love. When this belief was removed, her relationship with men improved dramatically.

We all have hidden beliefs and energetic programmes hidden in our bodies.

Every single friend, family member and encounter in your life is attracted to you by thoughts, beliefs and your unconscious patterning, which we have discussed. They must be unconscious if you find yourself in a situation similar to Kim's. Who would consciously choose to be unhappy, in an unloving relationship, working an unfulfilling job, with no money or hating life? Your unconscious energies and beliefs from others, often your parents, are running in your body, much like a virus in a computer. Like a computer virus, these energies can eventually cause your system to crash. This can manifest through the genetic blame game.

What is the genetic blame game?

Within the fields of therapy and energy it is all too easy to get caught up in people's problems. This is good for understanding the causes of certain things, but not so good for getting great results in your life, unless the process causes a swift, radical and permanent shift in focus afterwards. Because energy follows thought, all focus on a problem can often create more problems. Your parents always act in your best interests, to the extent of their abilities, beliefs and programming.

Blame can lead to pain.

Whenever I have taken people back to have a closer look at challenging family situations, there is always a link. When parents did not give as much love as their children would have liked, often **they** did not receive it from **their** parents. Just how many generations this pattern goes back is anyone's guess. Because you healed your parents and took on board their energies, it is highly probable you will develop some of the same habits. This can lead to the same diseases and outcomes for the next generation(s), unless you identify the problem, learn the lesson and change your belief around it.

Pain can lead to anger.

This is probably the most shocking part of my journey but I want you to know the blame game can kill you from the inside. At my angriest, most disillusioned point I had been triggered in a way I did not know was possible.

There was a time when I believed my life would be better if someone in my family was dead. I was not planning a murder or to personally inflict any harm on anyone, though I did feel if anything was to happen then I would be greatly relieved. I had reached my breaking point and could see no good reason why I should ever want to spend any more time with this person ever again.

My one redeeming point was I never said it to them. It only lasted for a few minutes but I was running energetic patterns inside me I did not know how to control and they were not even mine.

Anger can lead to guilt.

When I stopped running this pattern I started to feel very bad about ever not caring whether one of my family members was dead or not. I looked to justify this pattern logically but there was no logical explanation. I had moved from my usual, laid back, friendly, harmonious self to demonstrating traits of a raving lunatic.

Guilt can lead to lunacy.

To think energetic patterns inside me had the power to lead me to not caring whether someone died or not, scared me. This same thought was spiralling around in my head, consuming my life. If you have ever experienced, unproductive, guilty, consuming thought running around in your mind, then you have an idea of what I am talking about.

I'm talking about the feeling that happens when someone deliberately aims to play on your guilt, looking to manipulate you into a situation which feels awful to you. This was as close as I had been to insanity and I grew up in an asylum surrounded by it. It eventually helped me to realise I needed to invest time and money into finding out how this could happen. I was feeling like I had crossed the line. Was I going insane? This did not feel good to me.

Lunacy can lead to freedom.

Very few people I know have the capacity to take stress continuously and offload it, without being affected. This is a skill and an art. Often, it is the fear of what other people think preventing people from being who they really are, and doing what they really want to do.

There were hundreds of conversations/therapy sessions where I have worked with people who put on a strong front in one environment (often a work situation) and then gone home and crumbled. The energy of putting up a different face in one situation is a bit like wearing a mask. It can be utterly exhausting and this disparity will almost certainly lead to a total meltdown at some point. Fear of others seeing your real side at work can be crippling.

This fear has the power, if you let it, to turn your life into a prison, as you carefully hide your true feelings and desires from the rest of the world. Extreme stress can cause a jailbreak of repressed emotions, which get stored in the body when being someone else/putting on a front in certain situations for long enough. At this point, you may well be considered anything from not well to a raving lunatic, as others see you acting 'out of character.' Really, you are being true to yourself and accessing your real self, rather than the guarded, masquerade you may have spent most of your life showing up as.

Although it is fear rather than other people keeping you from this place of authenticity, often this fear is banished as your stress level reaches breaking point. When stored for too long this can appear like a volcanic eruption. In this case the wrong person says something at the wrong time and it causes an explosion.

This isn't about just one thing; it's about the hundreds or even thousands of small things that people have done to you along the way that have led you to a point of expressing yourself strongly. From this place, it can be devastating if the wrong person is the one on the receiving end when the explosion erupts. This is the moment your self-destruct button gets triggered.

It's a bit like an emotional version of pass the parcel. Your resilience/ tolerance represent people upsetting you whilst the music plays. When your resilience/tolerance run out, the music stops and you erupt at the person who happens to be the final trigger. If this is your boss, it could lead to the sack. If it's one of your family, it could be just as devastating unless properly resolved. Either way, the person who gets the first eruption will be left wondering what hit them.

It is a lot easier to express your real self from this place, without concern for what anyone else thinks. Having the courage to say what you really mean, do what you really want and live a life you really love can often appear as lunacy to anyone who is used to the person you had been showing up as. Being able to do this before you erupt is one of the biggest ways to avoid your self-destruct button. This represents freedom for many people.

Freedom can lead to change.

There are two courses of action from this point of breaking through your fears of other people's judgements. The first happens when you focus on what you don't want and how you will never let it happen again. This can manifest as reckless abandon and this can lead you to admission to an asylum. Here you will be subjected to an impressive array of random pharmaceuticals that may or may not help you to feel calmer. You will not have to deal with your life if you don't want to and you can literally drop out of society. Just watch the film *One Flew Over the Cuckoo's Nest* for an idea of what this can be like.

The second course of action is to connect with this intense pain and alchemise it. This is done by channelling your newfound receptivity to change, and following your heart. This occurs by using your Emotional Guidance System, until you are able to find what you really want and reach a place of feeling better. This was the path I chose. I made a commitment to myself to do whatever it took to create harmony in my life. I didn't know exactly what I wanted, I just knew I wanted to feel better and this was my goal. From here, I focused on positive outcomes.

In total, I spent about £100,000 on treatments, courses, books and answers. From spending time with Witch Doctors in South Africa, to discovering how to channel wisdom from my higher self using visualisation and sacred geometry. I learned more about energy healing systems, coaching, yoga, meditation, hypnotherapy, Time-Line Therapy, Neuro-Linguistic Programming and some courses so far out there they would not have been out of place within that asylum. I also realise that if I had read this paragraph before getting on this path I would probably be running in the opposite direction right now!

Only through seeing some of the things I talk about would I have ever believed them.

There was nothing I was not prepared to investigate to make myself well again and find what my heart was calling for. After all, now I felt I had ventured into the world of insanity, I no longer cared about how I was judged by others. From this place came an overwhelming sense of freedom and relief, married with a fearlessness I had never experienced before. My fearlessness was somewhere between letting go and having a reckless disregard for my own life. Retrospectively, it was self-sabotage and reckless abandonment masquerading as fearlessness. It was a fun adventure motivated by my own self-sabotage button being triggered. If someone told me not to go somewhere because it was dangerous – I was on my way to find out why!

The reckless disregard for my safety was due to another programme I was running unconsciously at the time, which was not revealed to me consciously until many years later, when I realised I had almost been aborted. I went backpacking all over the world, having new and exciting experiences. I sold everything I owned to facilitate this. I met new friends, visited incredible places and my life became a dangerously exciting adventure.

I had loaded guns pointed at me in Brazil and South Africa and was pursued in Cambodia by two men on a moped, one carrying an AK-47. I may well have set a speed record and certainly exceeded any best personal performance, by a considerable margin, that day. I witnessed hurricanes, earthquakes, riots and uprisings during my travels. I saw extreme poverty, which had me in tears, was shocked by my trip to the killing fields and the detainment complex in Cambodia, and took mind-altering drugs, some of which I had never even heard of before.

This world appeared a million miles from the structured, boring, high-pressure, repetitive emptiness my life had become back in England.

For the best part of ten years I found myself drifting from one healing system to another, never really finding anything that appealed to me in the long-term. I had all of the tools for change; I just wasn't using them. Because I had triggered my own self-destruct button I clearly didn't believe I was worthy of such tools, which I frequently used on others to get great results.

I kept asking myself how it was possible to have learned so many systems of healing, personal development, health and wellbeing and still not feel motivated to use any of them on any sort of sustainable level. What was the missing piece of the jigsaw?

Some people call this a mid-life crisis.

If you have been in the position where you start to feel restless and question everything in your life then you may know what I mean. For some it happens after decades of pursuing a career they thought would please their parents, even though they were never happy doing it. To others this happens with their personal relationships. They do not really love the person they are with but they are too scared to leave. Other people live highly successful lives, attracting wonderful relationships, well-paid careers and appear to have everything they ever wanted. Then they discover something is missing, but have no idea what it is. It's often a sense of purpose after already achieving everything they set out to do. This can create a feeling of emptiness despite all of their friends and family thinking that they are very lucky indeed.

Staying in this cycle can lead to depression. This is not good for your heart.

Depression is the calling of your heart for change as your head's decisions move further away from what feels good to you. Fortunately, I have always been more optimistic than most, fuelled by a sense of humour. Nothing beats being able to sit down with a good group of friends and discuss our neuroses. Being able to laugh at the quirks in our character and the situations life deals us is one of the most transformative things I know.

I know people who have worked both sides of the psychiatric divide. These friends are some of the best people I know and are fantastic with their patients. Empathy is often the missing link in many psychiatric settings and nothing prepares you better than seeing a service from the other side of the psychiatric divide.

Serendipity happens to those who expect it.

Travelling in countries where I didn't speak the language or know what was going on was a very scary and challenging thing at times, especially in some of the places and situations I ended up in. My dad always told me, 'If a genie appears and gives you one wish son, ask for luck.' I always have felt I was lucky and the more I think about it, the more it happens.

Back in 2007, my aunt needed somebody to look after her house for a few weeks, in Zakynthos, Greece. She lives on a mountain, looking down on a bay with bright blue water. It is a magical place, with wonderful energy. Suddenly, I left freezing, snow-swept England and arrived in a lovely, warm island paradise to contemplate my life and walk a dog for three weeks.

Then I had my 'Eureka!' moment.

I found myself putting together all of the pieces of the training I had done. Meanwhile, I went out walking for several miles every day with my new canine chum and returned each day feeling great.

I knew we all learn by association. All habits are learned this way. Ivan Pavlov proved this whilst training his dogs. Each time he was about to feed them, he would ring a bell. After a while, he would only have to ring a bell and the dogs would start to salivate. This was because they associated the bell ringing with food. This can happen to us as we walk by a bakery and smell the fresh bread. You may not have been hungry or even thinking about food but the smell of the bread may well have an association with eating for you.

Problems are also created by association. Just suppose you were listening to a certain song, just before something terrible happened, like a burglary, car crash or hearing news of the death of a loved one. You may not have been consciously aware of the role the song in question had in this process. Then suddenly the song plays again years later and you start to feel uncomfortable and fear starts to present but you have no idea why. The song is associated with bad things happening and unless you realise this consciously, you have associative programming in your system which does not help you.

How and where you learn is essential.

I thought about all of the things I had learned while being physically inactive throughout the process. If we are learning when we are physically inactive then we are associating the learning of new skills with physical inactivity. This is OK if you are training in Extra-Sensory Perception but not much good elsewhere.

If you have ever attended training or a class and learned potentially life-enhancing information but not used it then you will know what I mean. I knew Reiki could change my life and I had the proof, yet I wasn't using it. I knew hypnosis and Neuro-Linguistic Programming had the power to change my life, yet I wasn't using it. I knew Time-Line Therapy had the power to discover the root of my issues, yet I wasn't using it. I did use these techniques some of the time but not nearly as regularly as their results demanded.

How is it possible I could know so much and do so little?

All of these techniques and systems I had learned in a training room, whilst I was physically inactive. It dawned on me whilst I was in Zakynthos; I had spent a lifetime associating potentially life-changing information and techniques with being physically inactive. This had manifested throughout my life by finding I was always able to give everyone else great advice on any issue they faced, yet I was not putting this knowledge into practice in my own life. Have you ever noticed you doing the same thing?

Knowledge without action is not wisdom.

Knowing something can help you and not doing it can be more harmful than not knowing it at all. If you don't know what to do in order to make your life better then at least you would have a good reason for not getting better results in your life. When you know what you need to do in order to improve your life and do not do it then you also have the potential guilt and frustration to deal with, thus compounding the problem.

I wanted a better life but had been doing little about it.

Having spent so much money on my own education I needed to justify this to myself. I did this in Zakynthos by creating a system of integrating meditation and energy healing techniques into something I could do when I was walking. By taking all of the principles I had learned from the worlds of personal development and energy medicine, I started putting them into place as I went walking each day.

Now I found I was doing all of the things I knew would improve my life and associating them with physical action. Each day I would return from my walk filled with insight and the motivation to carry it through.

It was an enjoyable, energising process and allowed me to put all of my key learnings into a daily practice, without taking any time out of my day. I was able to turn every walk into a self-healing, self-discovery and self-help experience. The result was I became a walking energy dynamo, finishing each walk with more energy than I started it with.

Discover your path by what feels good.

It took an intense amount of pain to discover what I loved and create my own Active Energy System. This breakthrough was the single most powerful route to healing myself. Unlike anything else I had learned, during every walk I now associated mental action with physical action and started getting better results in my life. I became more focused, more motivated and more excited about my life.

I did not discover all of this on one trip to Zakynthos. I spent three years afterwards running walk-shops (walking workshops) for free because

I loved the process and wanted to share it. It was easy to do and I could associate powerful learning with physical action. I have had plenty more pain and numerous tests since this point, as I discovered the perils of going into business on my own. However, after a lifetime of dabbling with other things, I have finally found something I love. What is it you love to do?

I have been tested on many occasions during my journey and have been advised against teaching this system to others yet I keep being drawn back towards it as I learn to tune into the message of my heart. I just did not know how to market myself or my system very well during the early years. This, combined with a lack of confidence in my business skills, resulted in me ending up with no money and having to borrow from my family to even be able to afford to eat. This was a humbling place to be in my late 30s.

Despite this, I kept coming back to what felt best for me, believing in myself a little more each time. It's been an ongoing process and has hit many highs and lows. It has also seen me drift back into unhealthy habits and patterns on occasions; such is the rollercoaster of life.

What do you keep coming back to which feels good?

At the peak of my motivation I decided to write this book. Not because I thought it would ever make any money, but because it meant that if I were to die, there would be something useful left behind. I had sat down and written before, because I thought it would be a good idea. It was based on a thought, rather than a true feeling or passion to do so. I started writing this book ten days ago and have found each day when I sit down I can just write, without pausing and often without even thinking. This entire book was written in 28 days. What is calling you right now? What feels good to you?

My heart has guided me to share my message with you and call out to your heart's message which is waiting for you to discover it. If you have a big decision to make, write down all of your options and *feel* each one. To do this, think as if you had already decided to do each option, individually. How do you feel when you decide to go down a certain path?

Do you really mind what to do?

If you are like me, there will be occasions in life where you have asked someone a question, or they have asked you a question, where a choice is necessary. It can be anything from, 'What time do you want to go out this evening?' to

'Where would you like to go on holiday this year?' How often do you say or hear 'I don't mind', 'I don't care' or 'I'm not bothered?'

So often people pretend not to mind until a decision has been made by someone else they do not agree with. Often people have preferences but do not say, hoping the decision maker will be able to read minds. If you are uncertain of where to go on holiday, imagine a decision has been made for you to go to Spain and notice how you feel. Repeat this process with every other country you have considered and notice how you feel. If they all feel the same then it is OK to say you don't mind.

If a certain country appeals to you, even marginally more, then make a decision to go there. If the person asking you does not want to go there then you have a chance to get all of the real agendas out of the way, before the holiday has begun. This avoids statements like 'I didn't even want to come here in the first place,' being made once your holiday is in progress.

Get decisive.

Stay in permanent connection with your heart and know what *feels the best to you* at any given point. When you know this point then stick to it. Always respect the opinions of those who have your best interests at heart, yet give precedence to how you feel. If the advice of all of your friends is unanimous but it does not *feel good* to you then trust yourself and follow your heart. All great leaders were great leaders because they believed what others did not, did what all others did not believe was possible, faced doubt from the masses – but proceeded anyway.

And as a final note on this subject. Having worked with hundreds of people who were facing death and asking them what their biggest regrets were, it was always what they *didn't* do that caused the most pain, and very rarely something that they *did* do.

Exercise: Write down, right now 'The thing(s) that feel the best to me right now are...'

When you're done it's time to give you a word or two of caution.

Chapter 5

Making Sense of Your Biggest Challenges

Pain and death are part of life.

I realise this may take some of the magic and romance out of the journey but it is often the part that derails most people who decide to follow their heart. Just because you have found your true path and true message does not mean life will be easy because of it. Some aspects may be stressful and appear to make no sense when they happen.

Stress can be both your enemy or friend.

It is important to understand the role of stress in your life. Stress causes your body to go into fight or flight mode. When this happens, all other functions in your body are overridden and your body prepares you to deal with dangerous situations. This is your survival instinct kicking in.

Your body's stress response floods your body with adrenaline and cortisol, increasing your alertness and overriding fatigue. This causes your blood pressure to rise as the force of your heart's beat increases. This is necessary to get more blood and oxygen into your arms and legs. Your breathing rate increases to get more oxygen into your lungs. Your blood sugar increases, to supply your muscles. Your saliva dries up and your digestion and elimination systems are stopped so all available blood can be sent to your muscles and brain. Your reaction time improves, your muscles become tense and your sleep process is blocked. Also, your ability to take pain is increased.

This is a great response if you suddenly come across a wild lion in your daily life. It may not be enough to get out completely intact but it will certainly increase your chances of survival. Since there are not many wild lions in the average work office, then this is not such a great response when you are sitting at a desk and your life is not being threatened.

Your stress response is triggered with both real and perceived threats.

Whether you have a real threat to your life, or think about something stressful, your brain does not know the difference. You get the same fight or flight reaction whether you need it or not. Your stress response can be triggered by any thoughts causing you mental pain. This can range from criticism and being stuck in a bad memory, to having your job threatened, fear of redundancy, financial problems, being late and getting stuck in traffic. This is how road rage occurs.

When you spend increasing amounts of time worrying about things, it can cause you to spend more time in survival mode than is good for you. It is a bit like having a battery operated light and leaving it on when you are not in the room – you cause the energy supply to run out much faster than is strictly necessary. In this case the light represents your focus: you don't need it on when you are attempting to sleep. This is counterproductive and also the cause of insomnia.

In the same way that keeping a light on all of the time will end the life of the bulb sooner, stress-induced insomnia will end your life sooner if left unchecked.

Office worker's warning.

For an athlete or someone who needs to perform regular physical activity as part of their job, their bodies can burn up the excess sugar, fat and hormones. The stress response comes in useful when they are training and competing. For anyone who is inactive and having stressful thoughts then their body is full of hormones, stress and tension that do not get released. This is why people who have stressful office jobs are in more danger than most.

This can lead to agitation, digestion problems, loss of appetite, insomnia, fatigue, burn out, addictive tendencies, mood swings and predisposition towards depression.

Sustained stress is the biggest enemy of health and wellbeing for your heart.

Stress can lead to other lifestyle choices which do not always serve your heart. People who get stressed are far more likely to smoke more, drink more alcohol, make poor dietary choices and exercise less. Because of the peaks and troughs in energy the stress response leads to, it is highly likely stressed-out workers will finish their day with low motivation and energy. Any notion of exercise after work is less likely as a result. For this reason, it is essential to align your head and heart, thus reducing your predisposition towards stress.

When your head and heart align, nothing can stop you, except maybe death.

Let us take a look at some well-known people, who were clearly in alignment with the journey of their heart. The Dalai Lama, arguably the most well renowned spiritual leader alive today, talks about peace and happiness. When he was just a boy he was evicted from his own country after it was invaded and tens of thousands of his people were killed. There were even reports of Tibetan monks setting themselves on fire in protest. Because he is aligned with his heart, he chooses to use this incident to promote world peace and collaboration. Despite this, you can be sure there are those who do not appreciate his work.

Thomas Edison is another fine example of overcoming adversity. When his laboratories were almost destroyed in a fire in 1914, valuable records of his experiments and almost two million dollars' worth of equipment were lost. When surveying the damage he said there was great value in disaster as all of his mistakes are burned up. He also quoted, 'Many of life's failures were men who did not realise how close they were to success when they gave up.'

Harland David Sanders, perhaps better known as Colonel Sanders of Kentucky Fried Chicken fame, had his recipe for chicken rejected 1,009 times before a restaurant accepted it. Take a few seconds to think about this. Could you take over 1,000 rejections if you knew this was the price to make your mark on the world? How much belief must Colonel Sanders have had in himself to keep persisting?

Albert Einstein did not speak until he was four or read until he was seven, causing his parents and teachers to believe he was mentally handicapped, slow and antisocial. He was expelled from school and refused entry to Zurich Polytechnic School. Not exactly the start you may have expected for someone who went on to win the Nobel prize and change the face of modern physics.

Socrates was known as an 'immoral corruptor of youth'. Despite this, he is still regarded as one of the greatest philosophers of the Classical era and went on teaching right up until he was made to poison himself.

Wolfgang Amadeus Mozart began composing at the age of five, composing over 600 pieces of music, acclaimed as some of the best ever created. However, during his lifetime he was often restless, which led to him being dismissed from his position as court musician at Salzburg. He struggled to keep the support of the aristocracy and died with little to his name. Yet, he was inspired to keep composing during his life and has left a musical legacy for us all to enjoy.

Great people always face great adversity.

There are many examples from history of people who faced extreme adversity, yet went on to make an impact on the world, leaving legacies remembered long after their death. None of these inspirational individuals had an easy time. In his autobiography, Gandhi talks about his early years in South Africa, when he was looking to get fairer treatment after being thrown off a train for being Indian. At one point, he had an angry crowd, fuelled by incorrect media reports, waiting to lynch him. He could have avoided it but chose to face the crowd, where he was badly beaten.

So many examples can be gleaned from those who were really connected to their heart. The fire of injustice or ignorance often fuels a person's sense of purpose. They can connect to this and use it to fuel them when the going gets tough. Through having this connection in place, it is possible to overcome even the most difficult of challenges.

Belief in yourself is paramount.

There is nothing to substitute self-belief if you are to find a path in life you will pursue until the day you die. If you do not feel a burning desire to pursue a course of action for the right reason, then you will probably get derailed and not bother picking yourself up at some stage of the journey. If your heart is not calling so loudly you are able to pick yourself up and dust yourself down regularly along life's path, then the odds are you do not yet believe in yourself or your vision enough yet. From here, you either need more belief or a more compelling purpose.

But Adam, maybe my purpose was never meant to be big.

This is a fair point. Your purpose may appear relatively small. What if your purpose was to positively influence the next world leader? If you have children in your life then living a heart-based lifestyle may just give someone of the next generation the tools and belief to positively influence the planet. People, especially children, do not learn from words, they learn from actions. If you want someone to do something different for their own good then do it yourself and wait until they are inspired to do the same thing.

Alexander the Great is perhaps one of the most well renowned leaders in history. By the age of 30, he was the ruler of one of the largest empires in ancient history. However, it was his father, Philip, who set the foundations of his legacy. He united Macedonia and conquered Greece, whilst training Alexander and arranging some of the best tutors of the era to educate him. Amongst his tutors was Aristotle. Without Philip's foundation, Alexander would never have been in the position to do what he did. Heroes with lower profiles will usually surround every great leader. This may be your role and it is every bit as important and significant as those who lead.

Pain usually motivates more than pleasure.

For me and from my experiences of dealing with thousands of people who were ill, I have discovered pain is often a more compelling motivator than pleasure. I have touched upon this earlier. How then are you to use this knowledge to get in touch with your desire to be true to your heart and make a meaningful impact on the world?

When I first left my job as a nurse and decided to take an alternative path, I realised I needed to have a compelling and worthwhile vision in order to motivate myself everyday. I created a vision board and put all of the aspects of my vision upon it. I was going to teach over one million people my Active Energy System in three years. Simultaneously, this would fund the purchase of deforested land at the edge of rainforests I could use to start building up them up again.

With a vision this big and worthy, surely I would wake up motivated and filled with energy each day? For many days, I did wake up motivated and buzzing about how I was going to change the world. On other days, I would take such a battering emotionally as things did not appear to go my way, it was sometimes difficult to get out of bed in the morning. Do you ever have such days?

I had no idea what could be missing to give me the energy and motivation I needed.

From someone who was going to teach people how to get more energy and motivation with my Active Energy System I appeared to be facing a paradox.

Why wasn't I feeling energised after continuous rejection in the world of business? I clearly was not marketing my message in a way people would want to use my services.

From the sublime to the ridiculous.

I decided to go networking at one of my local groups and sell people on the benefits of learning a system to make them feel better more of the time and have more fun. They could learn it once and have it for the rest of their lives. My marketing strategy back then was pretty random and I changed it many times along the way. I had no idea what made people take action and was prepared to give anything a go. I even ran my walk-shops for free, hoping to entice people along. Little did I know at the time that I was building an idea on a terrible foundation.

The city I lived in at the time was St Albans. Traditionally, St Albans is a very conservative area. Having someone like me, who is a bit different, was always going to be a most interesting experience. One morning at a local network meeting, we were asked to pair up and talk to the person next to us about each other's business. I sat next to a chap who told me about his job, working in a firm who designed chocolates with company logos on them. His passion for his job did not exactly ooze out and when I asked him what his vision was he simply glazed over.

I told him I taught people how to increase their health through using Active Energy and find more meaning in their lives. I realise now this was not the best of tactics, as I had not identified a specific pain that I resolved for people. However, I thought by explaining my global vision, to help the planet, he might have had cause to find out more about me and what I did. After all, I had listened attentively to his passionless presentation about his job.

Then came the moment of truth.

We were asked to stand up and tell the rest of the group what we had just learned about the person sitting next to us. I stood up and did my best to explain companies could benefit from working with my partner for this exercise by creating a great impression through having chocolates with their logo on it for their guests and customers.

When my partner stood up to talk about my business, he told the group I was a bit of a hippy who was looking to save the planet. This did nothing for my credibility or business at the time, though it did make a few people laugh. Have you ever felt you were not being taken seriously?

Realising the distinct possibility people may not take my business seriously at this networking group from this point on, prompted me to take a more radical, alternative approach to it. For the next meeting, I dressed up as a hippy in my brightest collage of colours, wore a long wig, green glasses and a peace necklace, and set off to the poshest hotel in St Albans for our morning network meeting.

I walked in, put on an accent and started introducing myself as Ric, from Walk Innovation, my company name at the time. I said Adam couldn't make it today but I was here to talk about his business. The looks and responses I received from the rest of the group and the various commuters on my way in are still in my mind today. I had so much fun when I just decided to be someone else and lose all of my fear around networking.

My one-minute pitch received the loudest ovation of the morning, and some of the group did not realise it was me. Some of the looks I was given were priceless as I continued to play the part of Ric the Hippy, on a mission to save the world.

What did I learn from this Tomfoolery?

As a direct result of my actions I safely positioned myself as someone who was good fun, popular, a great person to talk to and someone a few of them would like to find out more about. I had a few opportunities but, because my marketing was vague I gained no business from it. I did gain a few friends and became popular on social gatherings but this was not what I was there for. This was all because I lacked confidence and self-belief. Coming out of the world of nursing straight into the world of business is not something I would recommend without some sort of training.

**My confidence had taken a knock and I was being tested.
From this point, I started to question myself and wonder what
I needed to do to make my business work.**

Maybe you have had one of those moments when you start to doubt whether you have what it takes. I was at this juncture. I then met someone from a much larger and more successful business than mine and set about doing things to add value to their business so they would help me with mine. My conversations with the owner involved great talk about win-win partnerships and everyone coming out of the equation smiling. This sounded good to me.

I introduced them to potential clients, and many great contacts in the speaking and promoting industries I knew. I also represented them in my own time and even lost over £3,000 in a joint venture where they failed to deliver on their side of the bargain, leaving me to mop up all of the expense. I had to borrow money to pay for it. Meanwhile, I had been recommending people to them and they were failing to deliver, harming my reputation.

Each time things did not work out I would hear some more great, rousing talk from the owner of the organisation. Usually around how we could all learn and move forward in a way we all gained. I was told I had not been clear in my communications and needed to learn from this. I was angry and my heart was telling me to cut loose but a close friend stopped me from cutting my association, in case anything positive could be gleaned from the situation. I swallowed my pride and suspicions that they were not acting in my best interests and had lied about promoting our event to their database, and did my best to see if we really could reach a win-win situation.

Even though I was feeling undervalued and unappreciated, I was still prepared to see if we could reach a mutually acceptable working relationship. They did offer me one day of work, where I would earn the princely sum of £100 after my expenses had been taken into account. It took them almost two months to credit my account, causing me to go into debt. I was at my lowest ever financial point here and every £100 counted. Have you ever pursued something even though your heart keeps telling you it wouldn't work out?

I needed more pain to believe in myself and do what needed to be done.

A few months later, after investing a significant amount of my time to promote them and build a workable relationship with this organisation, they delivered one final, crushing blow. I had been preparing a Heart Stress Prevention Workshop, which would educate corporate teams about the work-related causes of heart disease and how to reduce them. I thought we would be working in collaboration and had been guided to believe if I created these programmes they would market them to their clients.

The organisation's communications officer asked me to put a promotional video together to help promote my courses. I had to do this quickly as they wanted to send it out to their database in their next newsletter. I did as they asked, dedicating a full day of my time to the project. The communications officer received my video, sent the newsletter out without including any of my material and went on holiday, without telling me why.

I wrote to the owner of the place in question and received the only honest communication from them I would ever get. They had no intention of promoting my brand as it made no commercial sense to them. Their plan was for me to develop my content, give it to them for free and promote it under their brand.

I was furious.

I had spent the best part of a year promoting a bigger brand, for no money. They were not prepared to promote me but were prepared to lie to my face. I was fuelled with a fire, the like of which I had never known before. I felt used, deceived and bitter. Our relationship had been all about me giving and them taking and what was worse was I, a supposed heart health expert, had ignored all of the messages from my heart that this relationship had not been working for a very long time.

I removed the links to them from my website, removed all association with them from my social profiles and removed their phone numbers from my phone. I even removed the foreword they had written for my e-book, about The Active Energy System. When I had done this, I felt lighter, happier and more determined than ever to pursue my current vision with single-minded belief and determination.

Interesting that the company involved got paid to help companies to manage their stress!

It was the singularly most stressful business lesson that I would ever learn. The irony was not lost on me but I still hadn't had enough pain to get me angry enough to believe in myself. Therefore the lessons had to continue.

It was, however, this incident I have to thank for giving me the fire to motivate me to write this book in such a short period of time and start asking some of the wonderful people in my life for help. People and resources were all surrounding me, just waiting to be asked the right questions. I just did not have the belief, and focusing on a global vision was not enough to fuel this. I needed pain! Have you ever subjected yourself to unnecessary pain after not following your heart or properly believing in yourself?

However, the feeling of injustice allowed me to get really passionate about writing, and proved to be far more motivating than all of the positives. I knew enough techniques to release stress to let go, resolve and move on from this incident quickly. This has proved to be both a gift and a curse. It's been a gift in being able to manage my own stress in almost every situation I've ever been in. It's been a curse because it has kept me from being angry enough to do what was necessary to believe in myself.

It is only through living this issue myself that I was able to identify it in others. Too much confidence can lead to arrogance, which I find repellent. However, too little confidence leads to a lack of self-worth and a disastrous business owner, which is what I had been for most of my business life.

Pain can be motivating but being good at managing stress can be a barrier to it.

Being stubborn and good at managing stress can be a barrier to accessing self-belief. I needed someone to do something terrible to me in order to trigger my motivation strategy, a subject we will address in the next chapter. For this reason I am now very grateful to the organisation in question. Love was not enough to motivate me, I needed a kick up the backside and they gave me what I needed.

Even the most testing, painful of circumstances can have the power to either help you realise you are on the wrong track and highlight a need for you to change direction. Or they can help you realise you are most certainly on the right track and fuel you with an unstoppable fire you did not know existed within you.

Exercise: Remember your three greatest achievements in life and then think about what incident really drove you towards achieving them. Not the logical aspect of the equation but the thing that really stuck in your mind when you appeared down and out. Were these things pain or pleasure based?

Now you know this, we can take a more detailed look at your motivation strategy.

Chapter 6

Know Your Motivation Strategy

What gets you motivated?

You will never help yourself, help others or change the world in a positive way unless you have the motivation to do it. In order to do this you will need to understand your motivation strategy. Whilst we have already covered areas pertaining to this, now we will take a deeper look at motivation and how you can access it. Right now, you may well be wondering how it is possible for you to know so many great things which could improve your life, and do so little. This is very common. As I have already discussed, knowledge only becomes wisdom with action. And only self-belief can fuel wise action.

The stick versus the carrot.

There are two main strategies guiding us, which were touched upon in the previous chapter. One is the motivation of moving towards a goal because it is utterly compelling, feels great and you have an incredible urge to do it. This is a *towards* motivation strategy, or the carrot. The other motivation strategy, which I have found is far more common, is the *away-from* strategy, or the stick. This is where your motivation is pain-driven and you are finally motivated because you have had enough. In much the same way as you do not see jockeys riding with carrots dangling in front of their horses, the stick tends to be more effective in getting results.

If you did the last exercise then you will have an idea of what motivates you. Let us take an example of pleasure versus pain. For many years, I had been told of the benefits of meditation. People I had met who meditated regularly all appeared much calmer and more serene than most. The evidence was incredible. I knew meditation would improve my health and improve my life but I was too busy doing other things to care enough. I had known about the ten-day, silent meditation retreats they ran in Thailand when I was living out there. However, the idea of eight hours a day sitting down in a meditation position, a bed with a bamboo mat, wooden pillow and blanket, 4am starts, only two meals per day, no reading, no writing and no speaking, had made me reluctant to do it.

It was by being woken up as I slept in my beach hut, next to the sea on the Thai island where I was staying, to be told about a tsunami, that I started to receive alternative motivation. As relatives phoned up to find out whether I was OK and I watched clips on the news, I started wondering what would have happened if I had been on the west coast of Thailand instead of the east. I saw images of utter carnage, dead bodies floating around and survivors looking on as everything they owned had been washed away. The fact I wasn't there was down to chance. I was on Koh Samui, less than 100 metres from the beach. Our trip had taken us to the affected areas but not when it hit. Just weeks separated us from being in a tsunami-affected island.

I had been drinking large amounts of alcohol until 6am and would almost certainly not have made it out. In the state I was in, I may not have even regained consciousness. I started to wonder what I would have achieved if I had died that day, and I came up short.

This incident, motivated by the pain that I could have been dead and not achieved anything of real significance, made me realise that there was no time like the present to learn meditation. It was not as though I had not received similar warnings in the past. What was I playing at? I swiftly booked myself on the retreat that New Year's Eve. Just before I left, a very good friend, who was upset that I would not be joining him for a New Year's celebration, told me that I was mad and would not be able to keep my mouth shut for ten minutes, let alone ten days. He said he was sure that I would be back after two or three days, regretting missing New Year's Eve.

Pain motivates.

I was woken at 4am every day from my bed of a concrete mattress with a bamboo mat, blanket, mosquito net and wooden pillow. I was not allowed any phone, reading or writing materials or any other form of distraction. I was forced to be there with just my thoughts.

During that ten-day period, especially during the first five days, there were several occasions where the intense pain sitting down, cross-legged, for over eight hours per day was almost unbearable. As my knees, hips and lower back were screaming out for me to quit, I would just visualise the smug look on my friend's face about me not lasting ten minutes, let alone ten days. This enabled me to take a little bit more pain and kept me going that extra mile.

I repeated this strategy on numerous occasions during this particular retreat and by day nine I finally started to understand that, as I had been instructed, my physical pain was just a reflection of my mental pain. The last two days were relatively easy and extremely energising for me. I had been in so much pain that it filled me with gratitude to finally experience the feeling that can happen with meditation when time appears to distort and great insight is reached.

Test this yourself.

Pleasure is clearly not a motivation for people who want to lose weight but have tried many diets, each one failing to help them. If the thought alone of having a body like a model, improved confidence, relationships and longer and happier life was enough for people to lose weight then nobody would be fat. As it turns out, in the UK alone it is estimated that 43% of males and 33% of females are overweight. In the US it is estimated that one-third of the population are obese.

Pleasure is simply not as motivating as pain for most of the population.

Having spoken to a number of good martial artists, often it was the experience of being beaten up as a child that motivated them to excel at their art. There are also some big brands which were motivated by pain. Timothy Martin named his famous pub chain after an old school teacher. That was how J. D. Wetherspoon was born. Timothy describes his old teacher as, 'The least likely person to control a pub because he couldn't even control a class.' Who would have thought that doing such a bad job could make you the name of a large brand?

I have known people who wanted to give up smoking for years, telling themselves, 'I just don't have the will power.' Then they give up the minute that they found out that they were diagnosed with cancer. Another friend of mine was driven to give up after years of struggling, by his daughter refusing to kiss him when he smelled of cigarettes.

All pain is attracted into your life to help motivate you to listen to your heart's message.

I realise that this statement has the potential to open up some very long and heated debates. What about people who are born with disabilities? What about torture, violence and hate? What about abuse, rape or mistreatment of children?

People who have been hurt the most often have the power to help more people.

I realise these are sweeping statements. Happiness and love are both wonderful to experience. They can make your heart sing with joy. They are your key to increasing your chances of living a longer, happier and more purposeful life. However, in much the same way as Dr David Banner did not always get what he wanted in his normal, everyday life, sometimes he had to get angry before people started to take him seriously as he became the Incredible Hulk!

Whilst I am not advocating that you paint yourself green and start ripping off your shirt every time someone upsets you, I am saying that painful situations have just as important a role in your life as the pleasurable ones. They are not better or worse, just necessary to trigger some people's motivation strategy. If you are currently not feeling in love with yourself and in love with your life then it may just be a case that you have not had enough pain to trigger your motivation strategy.

Most people are oblivious to pleasure.

The word 'most' has been used before in this book, so let me clarify exactly what I mean: more than half.

So often, when I listen to people bursting at the seams to tell me how a certain situation is unfair, unjustified or not good enough, I watch them as they come alive, filled with injustice. I never see these same people get so passionate about what they love or want to attract in their lives, yet annoy them and they become fuelled with energy. For anyone listening to such angry rants, it is likely you will take on board some of this angry energy unless you have set your energy field not to.

Fortunately there are techniques to clear any energy that is not yours. If you are not trained in setting your energy field then you are likely to attract other people's angry energy, fears and limitations as they offload on you. Because your energy field is magnetic it is likely you will attract the energetic patterns of those who you spend the most time with. This can then cause you to offload on someone else. We will discuss this further in the next chapter.

You may be thinking, 'Oh no, so it's because I spend so much time with _____ that I feel this way.' This is not the whole truth. The blame game is a boomerang: once you throw it out there it will always come back and hit you, usually when you least expect it. If you are spending time with people who continuously offload their problems, drain you or give very little back then it is likely that you need much more pain in order to really understand the bigger picture: that you are a fantastic, wonderful, loving and infinite being, who is here for a bigger reason than you can possibly imagine right now. You just need to be awakened and start to own your power.

Blame creates more pain.

Blaming anyone else but you for what isn't working in your life will take you away from the message in your heart and move you slowly towards a miserable death. There is no nicer way to say it. When you hear people talk about energy vampires then they are in just as much danger of missing the point of life as those whom they accuse, if not more so.

Think of the best films, stories or fables that you know of. Which are the ones that have really inspired and/or moved you? Were they tales of someone who was given a silver spoon, did not have to do anything and had a happy life, or those who spent their lives complaining about others and how bad their life is? Or were they tales of extreme persistence, challenge, and overcoming adversity, where only through an iron will, dogged determination and unshakeable belief, did the hero pull through?

Know what you want in life that would make everything else seem justified.

When I truly started to believe that I was here for a bigger purpose than I would ever have dared to dream about before, my issues became easier to resolve. All of my family challenges made sense and I was able to resolve them. The people who had done terrible things to me, abused my trust, hurt me for no good reason and actively attempted to make my life difficult, all suddenly became my teachers, friends and guides. Every incident in my life had been training me to accept the inevitable criticism that comes with being in the public eye, with a message that will make a lot of other experts in the field very uncomfortable.

Everyone in your life is there to help you to discover your true calling. If you are moving towards a place that feels good to you, then the people in your life will probably be mainly very supportive. If, however, you are not being true to your heart then people will be drawn into your life to increase your pain, in order to motivate you to change. They are not bad for you unless you let them be so. They are just doing what is necessary to trigger your motivation strategy and get you to listen to your heart's message.

As a person with a generally laid back demeanour, I was able to take small slights in my stride, whilst being blissfully unaware of the bigger picture. I was too busy having fun and experimenting with drugs to even consider that I needed more pain to help me to realise this. Does this ring a bell for you?

Learning about advanced stress management techniques made me quick to forgive, when others may have lost the plot. Being ripped off and having my reputation tarnished unfairly by a business mentor after I had paid him £15,000 was tough to take. Him refusing to give me a refund after acting unethically in a way that cost me business outside of the training room was a lesson that took me a long time to let go of the negativity surrounding it. It ultimately led to me having to move, as I was clearly fighting a fire that I could not see. Clients left as a direct result of his actions and nobody said why. I came back home to find my house burgled and the door smashed in.

This might have triggered an angry response for most but I was quick to see the positive in everyone and everything. I still wasn't getting the bigger picture and letting myself access the pain in my life. I thought I was being spiritual by doing nothing about these things. I was delusional! My lack of self-belief was blocking me from getting the message.

When you stop yourself from feeling the pain in your life then you will attract increasingly testing situations to help motivate you.

I had to wait years to find myself broke and in a situation bad enough to make me face up to the fact my life was not working and I was not truly happy. It took me to a situation where I couldn't even afford to feed myself, to become angry enough to start demanding I was taken seriously and change the rules in my life. As I listened to people who drove expensive cars and lived in expensive houses tell me they could not afford to pay me for helping them to clear their energy, I started getting really mad. I cut all of the ties that didn't feel good.

I had valued myself so little that empty promises and good talk, accompanied by poor action, had sustained me on my quest to make my business work. I had wasted months of my life with people who were not taking me seriously and missing opportunities with those who would. The fact was that these people were all attracted into my life to help me to realise that this was not my path. Maybe you can relate to this place? Are you not giving yourself the credit that you deserve? And what are you prepared to do about it?

So often, when people start telling me their problems, I ask, 'What do you want?' Usually this leads to a response along the lines of 'I know that I don't want this to happen again,' or 'I want them not to ever speak to me like that again.' In both cases, and I could list hundreds of examples here, people often do not hear the question asked of them, as they are so wired into the problem. Frequently, I have to ask exactly the same question four or five times before I finally get to a response that is towards something positive. Knowing what you do not want does not set a route map towards what you do want.

An 'away-from' motivation can lead you anywhere.

Unless you have a bigger picture, positive, energising goal in your life then it is likely that you will spend most of it moving away from pain. The trouble with the strategy of moving away from pain is that without a positive goal, it can take you to an even more painful place. This can play out for the rest of your life. When you have no vision, purpose or ultimate goal then you will usually have a default setting of moving from one painful situation to the next. Meanwhile, your heart is attempting to trigger something bigger from within and hoping that it does not become necessary to attack you. Often this leads to serious disease.

Maybe you have had some of these experiences. If you have ever felt as though you were taken for granted and that this was a pattern in your life, then it may be time to start feeling more pain in order to motivate you towards positive action. It could be time to make you the most important person in your universe. If you have recently found out about a potentially serious medical condition then you most certainly need to not just *read* this section but to *feel* it.

Start using pain as your guide and friend.

If you are feeling a deep resentment, anger or injustice about anything in your life, then now is the time to associate with that pain and allow it to flow. Get angry, let loose and allow how you really feel to spill out until you are motivated to make the change that your heart is desperate for you to make.

Exercise: Ask yourself, 'What would I have to achieve in order to justify everything bad that has ever happened in my life?' If all painful situations were there to guide you to a better place then what achievement would it take to make all of the pain in your life worthwhile?

Now that we have looked at your pain, let us now look at how to set your energy field to clear dense energy and create a space of transformation.

Chapter 7

Setting Your Energy Space

We have talked earlier about how your energy field is magnetic and your thoughts influence your energy so now I am going to ask you to take a leap of faith and take control of your energy. I realise that this concept may not be exactly easy to comprehend but this stuff really works. Having tested this on numerous occasions, I can assure you that you can not only clear the energy of anyone who is offloading on you, as it happens, but you can influence who you attract towards you.

It was around 2008 that friends of mine told me to go and see a man called Art Giser, because he was teaching some incredible energy techniques. I didn't really feel drawn towards him at first, as I'd had so many energy teachers, all of whom had not impressed me, tried to complicate things or even said that I wasn't ready to know such things until signing up for their advanced courses. I had studied so many energetic systems and techniques that I wondered why I would want to invest my time and money in learning any more.

A serendipitous chain of events.

As it turned out, I was asked along to his training in order to give my opinion. During our first encounter, he stood in front of the group and explained that we all took on other people's energy because our energy field was magnetic and patterns and programmes within us attracted certain people and energies into our lives. When he asked us all how much of our current energy was our own, genuine energy, I guessed about 70%. Imagine my shock when I found out that it was nearer 3%.

His experience of reading people's energy field had shown him that 3% was about average for anyone who had never been taught how to clear their energy field. Then I thought about it; if my energy field is magnetic and I never knew how to clear it, then I had spent my whole life attracting unfiltered energy from everyone that I came into contact with. Art and I have since become good friends and he has taught me plenty about working with energy. I will offer you some techniques in this section that he has taught me and encourage you to look up Art if you wish to find out more about this fascinating field.

Energy follows thought.

Again, I will keep emphasising this point. Start by grounding yourself, which we have already talked about. This is the essential foundation for all work with energy. Because your energy field is magnetic, you can remove some of the energy that is not yours by simply imagining a lake in front of you, with a large, powerful magnet in it. Then just intend for any energy that is not yours to be drawn towards the magnet. You may see it or feel it, or you may not. Either way, just by intending it to happen, it will.

You can allow this to happen until you feel that the process is complete. Then imagine the magnet dropping into the centre of the Earth and dissipating. After that picture a ball of light above you beaming down white or gold energy through you and filling up all of the gaps left by this energy release.

Energy abhors a vacuum.

Have you ever thought that you had cleared an issue only to have it pop up again? If you have then you will know how frustrating this can be. One of the biggest mistakes that I had been making in my energetic journey, up until that point, was releasing energetic patterns, beliefs and issues, yet not replacing them with anything. From here, I used to be left wondering what I had to do to fully release my blockages.

By releasing energy that wasn't mine and not replacing it, I allowed more energy that wasn't mine back into my energy field. When I learned that I needed to think about my energetic space being filled up with white or gold light when I had finished releasing, everything started to change for me.

Get into the habit of releasing other people's energy regularly.

Your energy field is like a high-powered magnet moving through a metal store. You are constantly attracting things that may not be serving you when you don't set your energetic space. For this reason, it is good practice to start and/or end your day by running through the above exercise. You may not even believe that it works but because your energy follows your thoughts, it will work anyway, just by you thinking about it.

Set your energy field each day for what you want to attract.

I am not going to promise that you will only attract exactly the things that you intend to each day. What I am going to promise is that if you do, you will dramatically increase the likelihood of you getting it. Do your magnet exercise and fill your energy field up with light. Set your intention to dissolve anything else in your field and know exactly what you would like to attract more of during your day. Maybe it is opportunity, money, happiness, love, flow or luck.

Your Reticular Activating System (RAS)

Your RAS is what is activated when you set your intention towards something. If your RAS is set on spotting red cars, you will start to notice more red cars than you probably ever had before. This is not because there are suddenly more red cars, but it is because you are setting your focus to become more aware of their presence. Your RAS is like a heat-seeking missile – it keeps searching until it finds its target. Just imagine the opportunities that you may have missed by not tuning your RAS to become aware of them. When you do not set your RAS then it is possible that others may set it for you.

Think of a time when you were just sitting there, minding your own business and someone just sat down next to you and started to offload their problems onto you. You may have listened attentively, offering a sympathetic ear and good advice. At the end, it is likely that the person who has just dumped their problem on you feels considerably better and you may feel drained. Your RAS is now focused on someone else's issues because you have not set it to serve your needs that day. If you find that you are continuously attracting people in your life who share their problems and challenges, then this may well be down to you not setting your RAS.

Be more self-ish.

It is wonderful to want to help and serve others but you cannot give from an empty vessel. Only by putting your needs at the top of your agenda, every day, will you be able to help others more effectively. If you find yourself feeling drained after listening to others' problems then this section is particularly important for you. If you have set your own RAS that day to be energised throughout and you find yourself in a situation where your energy is draining, then have the courage to walk away. Apologise if you like, but get out of any situations that you do not have the energy to deal with.

As we have discussed earlier, people who are disconnected from their energetic source will feed off your energy for as long as you allow them to. This not only drains you but it doesn't really help them either, as they are still disconnected when they have finished draining your energy. Only you can allow this to happen and only you can stop it. People who are not connected to their source energy do what they need to energise. They have probably never been taught how to connect themselves to their source. If you feel your energy draining then walk away. Your real friends will always understand and rarely be offended. Anyone else clearly isn't worth it.

The problem-dumping survival guide.

If you are feeling energised enough to listen to other people tell you their challenges then here is a guide to keeping your field clear of toxic thoughts and energy. This explanation is a guideline for you. In all energy work that you do, I would suggest that you always follow your intuition and inner guidance. If you get an urge to use different shapes, colours, methods or intentions then I recommend that you trust yourself and notice what results you get.

First, as always, ground yourself and also intend for the other person to be grounded too.

Intend for your energy field to stay clear, and think about an energetic rod being between you and the person that you are with. Make it your intention that any energy relating to this issue that does not serve you in that moment goes straight into the energetic rod, which is connected to the centre of the Earth. You have now set a space, which supports both of you and will allow you to be in this person's presence, without taking on board any of their energy. When I do this process, I often intend for white light to fill the space (use white or gold if you are not sure what colour to use but trust your intuition if you get another colour). When you have finished just intend for the rod to move fully into the Earth and dissipate.

This set-up allows you to hold the space for people to voice their challenges and works better when you remain fully present and listen until a few seconds after they have finished talking. Effective communication is not just a great tool for any therapeutic process, it is a great tool for every interaction that you ever have. Using this opportunity to deepen your breathing allows you to use this time to raise your own energy, without being affected by any potentially toxic energies being released in this process.

So often I notice people just itching to talk as others speak, frequently interrupting mid-sentence. Listening is one of the best skills that you will ever develop. An InsBeCo global internet poll showed that 82% of people preferred to spend time with a good listener than a good speaker. When you become a good listener, others will want to hear what you have to say and be better listeners for you.

Clear and set the space of any room that you walk into.

It is possible for you to clear and set the space in rooms as you walk into them, in order to facilitate more favourable outcomes. In order to do this just intend for a grounding rod (make one up if you are unsure what one looks like) to be planted in the middle of the room and cords of energy connecting to it from all eight corners of the room (four on the floor and four on the ceiling.) Once this is set up, feel free to add any colours that you feel drawn to use. You can clear energy from a room by thinking about a big magnet, then dropping it to the centre of the Earth and letting it dissipate. This can be done in a car, on a bus, on a train or anywhere that has an enclosed space.

If you are outside then get creative. If you wish, you can just think about having a space filled with light surrounding you. I have found myself attracting some wonderful people in random settings by imagining myself giving off a purple flame. The limit to this is your imagination. Just remember to ground yourself before all energy work.

As with anything in life: you don't have to believe it and what you believe is more likely to manifest. If you don't believe it (and I certainly didn't when first introduced to this concept) then you have everything to gain by testing it.

Feeling is believing.

I realise that in this chapter I have possibly strayed off the path of what you may be ready to believe. As I said at the start of the book, I really do not want you to believe any of this, I want you to use it and then decide for yourself. Maybe you will not be certain that by setting an energy space you had any influence on how things turned out. That's OK. Just ask yourself whether you had a good experience after doing it. If the answer is yes then repeat it.

With your RAS focusing you on exactly what you want, and the ability to clear and set the energy of everywhere you go, you are now in possession of two of the best energetic tools that I know. The question that you are probably wondering now is 'Does this really work?' You may be thinking, 'Surely it can't be that easy.' Yes it does and yes it is are the answers. However, I will understand if you are not yet feeling confident enough to go out and do this. It took me many years to accept these principles. This is why I only encourage you to play with the ideas if you do not yet feel certain that they will work for you.

> *Exercise: What one thing, quality or opportunity would you attract into your life if you knew, for certain, that you would get it? When you know, write it down somewhere where you will see it every day and set your RAS to attract it. Be aware that this may take time but the more often you do it, the more likely that you will be ready for the moment when opportunity presents itself to you.*

Now that we have talked about setting your energy space, we will discuss the different levels of using energy to heal.

Chapter 8

The Different Levels of Energy

Different strokes for different folks.

I have studied many different healing systems. Reiki and Vortex Healing are just two that I am trained in. Both involve some complicated aspects that I was never quite able to come to terms with, so I did some research.

Fortunately, Energetic NLP and Art Giser made things much clearer for me. Some things are complicated for no good reason and there can be plenty of dogma and spiritual bigotry within the healing community. I am certain that we are all healers/energy givers. The only difference is that some of us know it and most of us don't. Your thoughts are energy. By thinking about someone, you can affect them.

Get your ego out of the way.

Working with energy can be a beautiful gift, or a can of worms when ego gets involved, especially to anyone who has trained to be a healer. If you have trained in any healing system that involves energy then the biggest mistake that I witness is healers thinking that they are providing the healing. It is my belief that none of us has the power to heal anyone who is not ready to heal themselves. Yes, you can provide the space for healing to occur and initiate the process, but you can never heal anyone else who is not ready. Even the word 'healer' used to feel uncomfortable to me.

When I first started giving energy treatments to my friends, family and patients I really didn't know if it was going to work and did exactly what I had been trained to do. I didn't believe that I was doing much to help and had no expectations. I was continually surprised that people were reporting positive outcomes after I had worked with them. During this period, other healers, who could see energy or get insights about the deeper problems involved, intimidated me. I could do none of this and would frequently doubt my ability and think that to be a good energy worker I needed to develop the ability to see energy or get insights on what was wrong. I had a case of energy envy. Consequently, I expected nothing from the process, yet achieved many great outcomes.

I have since come to learn that we are each just as gifted when it comes to working with energy. The biggest initial barrier is, believing in yourself. To compare your ability to someone else in this field is a bit like Superman losing heart in his ability because he cannot spin webs like Spiderman. We each have a gift that is unique to us. Comparing yourself to someone else is as pointless as it can be destructive.

Once you believe in your ability then the next biggest barrier is believing that you have more influence over the process than you actually do. Over time, my ego started to inflate and I started believing that it was me, and not the energy that I was channelling, giving this healing gift to those who I worked with. I thought that I had the power to heal everyone. When I did this, I also started questioning my ability if my sessions did not appear to be working, which will happen with any healer who is working on someone who is not ready or willing to be healed. We will discuss why this can happen in the next chapter.

After working with several of my patients on the ward, I realised that energy did not appear to work on the physical wellbeing of everyone, because I was expecting certain outcomes. Working with energy can manifest in many mysterious ways. For this reason, expecting certain results is not productive. There are different levels of healing, which I did not realise during my early days.

Everyone has the power to heal.

You may well ask, 'How is this possible when we all die eventually?' This is an excellent question.

Healing occurs on many different levels: physical, mental, emotional and spiritual. Healing is not just aimed at one or the other; it works exactly in alignment with what the person needs. I found this out by accident, years before I had ever heard about energy medicine.

Healing happens on different levels.

Back in 1997 I went to Australia with a year's working visa. During this time, I worked for nurse agencies in Melbourne, Perth and Sydney. The experience was a good one as I was able to see how another health care system worked.

During this period, a stack of interesting experiences occurred for me, though the most significant happened in Sydney. What happened here would alter my perception of life, healing and what nursing was all about.

Working as an agency nurse in a city usually means working at several different hospitals, in several different wards. This had been my experience after 11 months in Australia. Because the staff liked me, I'd been requested back to work on the same rehabilitation ward, in a private hospital, for several consecutive night shifts.

Since this ward was generally quiet for most of the night, I usually brought a book along with me to pass the time.

To find my next book I went into a second-hand bookstore and went to the spirituality section. I stood back and waited for a book to grab my attention. One soon did – *The Tibetan Book of Living and Dying* by Sogyal Rinpoche. I picked it up and started to read it that night.

The opening chapters explain, amongst other things, that the main difference towards death in the East and the West is that in the East people are generally prepared for death from a very young age.

The West has a general theme that we don't usually face up to death until it's staring us in the face. This resonated with me. How true. I had seen it on numerous occasions – scared patients and hysterical families attempting to make sense of the impending demise of a loved one after a doctor had given them a death sentence.

I thought about this a lot during the next couple of nights.

During my time on this rehabilitation ward, I came to know the patients quite well. Each night I would stop in and have a chat with each of them, handing out the assorted pharmaceutical delights that they had become accustomed to.

One of my patients was a lady called Dorothy. She had fallen over at home several months ago. She had no medical history, just a case of bad luck. She had a lovely smile and a most pleasant demeanour.

After about eight shifts on this ward, I went in one night to be informed that Dorothy would be going home the next day. I entered her room last that night so that I could have a longer chat with her, beyond the cursory five minutes that we usually had.

'Congratulations. You must be delighted,' I told Dorothy, as I walked into the room.

'Huh! Delighted? What possible reason would I have to be delighted?' Dorothy was unusually curt in her response.

'I don't understand. Are you not happy to be going home?' I asked.

'What have I got to be happy about? I live on my own and I can barely make it from the bed to the toilet. I'm dependant on someone else to do my washing, cleaning, shopping and cooking. I can't ask my daughter to look after me – she has enough on her plate. She has two young children and a very demanding job. I have absolutely nothing to look forward to.'

Upon hearing this from this sweet, usually smiling, old lady, I found myself momentarily speechless. I had not expected that from her. My mind went blank.

After a prolonged pause, I asked her, 'Do you believe in life after death?'

Then it was Dorothy who paused, before looking me in the eye and saying, 'Well, I'd like to but I just don't know.'

This prompted a discussion about life after death and some various perspectives that I'd come across at that stage in my life. We talked for well over an hour and a half. I mentioned the Dalai Lama being reincarnated several times and that this was fact according to millions of Buddhists across the world. I'd also heard about a Native American Indian ritual whereby people knew they were about to die and sat around a campfire and gave all of their worldly belongings away. This was their way of cutting the ties with this world and moving on to the next.

I surprised myself at the depth of information I had acquired over the years about alternative beliefs about dying and psychic occurrences indicating strongly that death is not the end. I had not thought about it too much before – but given the choice between life after death and no life after death – I knew which one I preferred the sound of. Despite this, I wasn't sure either.

At the end of our chat, Dorothy grabbed my arm and her face lit up. 'Thank you Adam, this has been the most useful conversation that I've ever had.'

Her words touched me, though I thought little of it at the time. She had been experiencing anxiety and I had said something to alleviate it. I'd done this numerous times before. I wasn't really sure about what I'd told her but she seemed happy enough, so my job was done.

I looked in her room before leaving the next morning but Dorothy was sound asleep, so I left the ward and went home.

That night I went back into the same ward. As I arrived, there were doctors running down the ward and into the room that Dorothy had been in. I wondered what was going on, as she should have been discharged. I slowly made my way to the room and Dorothy was flat on the floor and the medical team were attempting to resuscitate her.

I went numb as I witnessed the futile attempts of the team to resuscitate her. Dorothy had no medical history – this was out of the blue. There had been no warning, no plausible medical explanation and no reconciling the distraught nurse who had been looking after her during the day. She told me that Dorothy had told her just 20 minutes before she died that 'I feel better than I have done in years.'

I'd helped Dorothy die and I was the only one that knew it.

Physical healing was not what Dorothy had been looking for: it was spiritual, mental and emotional healing that she needed. As I watched the resuscitation team in action I felt a resounding peacefulness permeate my body. Had Dorothy waited for me to return to die? I'll never know this for sure. It's also worth noting that I had no training in any energy systems when this occurred.

What I do know is that this incident was the most profound one that I ever had as a nurse.

It was this incident that made me realise that healing goes way beyond the physical and if the healing of the physical body is the only focus of a healer or health care professional then they are in for a shock or two somewhere down the line.

I realise that this story is not exactly light-hearted but it is a true and very personal account of one of my earliest experiences of how healing can occur even minutes before someone dies. For this reason, looking at wellness on just a physical level can cause great pain for families and individuals facing death. Consequently, I intend only that I work in the best interests of anyone I give healing to, allowing light to flow into them. Whether they get any obvious benefits out of this is out of my hands. I now have no attachment to this. I also encourage you to lose all attachment from any outcomes when working with energy or other people.

Granting people permission to die.

Dorothy's case was the first of many in my understanding of the dying process. Even the most religious of people have confided in me as death becomes imminent that they are not sure about life after death. I have had so many talks with people and in many cases they are about to die but had never given it any serious consideration before.

I've witnessed people hold on until certain friends or family members arrived. Then watched them die within minutes of them leaving. Understanding the dying process and working with families through this is one of the most rewarding things I have ever done. This taboo area is one which causes the most pain for many if not fully understood.

If you are still grieving for a dead family member you will know exactly what I'm talking about.

Setting your energy space around loved ones who are about to die can be a powerful experience.

Much as I'd love to say that I hope you are never put in the position of being there during the final minutes of a loved one, this is not likely. When you understand a few basic principles, this can be one of the most powerful and rewarding experiences that you will ever have. I am here to tell you that this can be an incredibly healing experience for you and them, when you realise that you can help right up until the final moments.

Hearing is the final sense to go during the dying process.

So many times distraught relatives would ask me whether their dying family member would ever regain consciousness. I would always explain that hearing was the last sense to go. This allowed people to say what they wanted, creating a healing space and, usually, a much more favourable last memory. It is never too late to tell someone that you love them and it can never be said too often.

It is also important to know that energy does not require words. By setting your energy field around someone who is dying, you can help them, without even opening your mouth. Just thinking about what you want to communicate will work. Love is a good intention to hold at this moment. Often I would just sit and hold the hand of people who were about to die, setting my energy space to facilitate peace, love and healing.

> *Exercise: Get comfortable, ground yourself and set your intention to give yourself energy at whatever level is right for you now to become happier, healthier and more in alignment with the message of your heart. Then just imagine light entering your body, through your head and/or feet and filling up your energy space. Be sure to drink a large glass of water both before and after this exercise and be sure to write down anything that enters your awareness during this process, after you have finished.*

In the next chapter, we will look at the reason why many people are resistant to being helped at a physical level.

Chapter 9

Why Some People Don't Heal Physically

You may well be thinking that nobody would not want to get better, be healthier or heal themselves physically. I also thought this until I witnessed an increasing amount of situations that made me realise that some people can quite literally will themselves ill or even dead. Without mental or spiritual health, physical health can be meaningless. Reduced physical health can also be a gateway towards having mental and spiritual needs met. By focusing only on a person's physical wellbeing, you may be wasting your time and missing the point of the bigger picture at play here.

Secondary gain.

Most afflictions, illnesses and painful situations always have a benefit. This benefit I shall refer to as secondary gain. Secondary gain happens when someone receives something that they perceive, either consciously or unconsciously, to be more important than resolving an illness or problem.

Harold's case was very common. He had been living on his own for over ten years since losing his wife to a heart attack. He was able to just about cope at home but his life had become increasingly lonely because his relatives had not visited him in over seven years. He saved money on heating by using blankets and being a little colder than he would have liked in the winter, and hardly left his house because he was a little bit shaky and uncertain on his feet.

One day, during a very cold December, he suddenly developed pneumonia and was admitted to hospital. It was protocol to advise his next of kin that Harold had been admitted to hospital, in this case his nephew. He was taken to a warm hospital bed, surrounded by people to talk to and had company for the first time in many years. Nurses, doctors and physiotherapists fussed over him, bringing a smile back to his face.

The next day his nephew arrived, with his wife and young children. It was the first time that Harold had seen his two grand-nephews. They brought him fruit and chocolate and were full of apologies for not having visited him for so long. Suddenly, despite having not seen Harold for over seven years, his nephew was making frequent demands of the nursing staff. He demanded that Harold received the attention that he deserved. It never ceases to amaze me how relatives who neglect the elderly members of their family suddenly become extremely concerned for their wellbeing when they get ill and think that they may be close to death! Often high demands are made of the staff and difficult situations arise. This was very common during my time as a nurse.

One week later, just a few days before Christmas, Harold was told that he was well enough to go home. This caused his mood and energy to drop. He would be returning to his cold, empty house to once again, spend Christmas on his own.

Harold now had a taste of the mental and spiritual benefits of being ill.

Within one week, Harold was back with another infection. Was this bad luck or had he created an illness because of the secondary gain involved? If I had not witnessed at least one hundred very similar case studies over my nursing years then I may have attributed it to poor fortune. However, this was just one example of many.

The tragedy of this was that patients would often come back having fallen over and broken a bone, in some cases never to leave the hospital again. There reaches a point in many people's lives that they would rather be ill and have people near them than be well and on their own.

Often I witnessed couples who had been together for over 40 years die within weeks of each other. This happened to my grandparents. After 68 years of marriage, my grandad passed away when he was 94 years old. He had been laughing and joking on the ward the day before. The next day my granny had a heart attack. She would never recover or return home, dying a few short months later. My granny made it clear to me on numerous occasions that she did not want to live any longer. At 90 years of age, she felt that she had done what she came here to do.

This can also happen when people get stuck in problem cycles.

So often, I used to hear people tell me the same problem time and time again. I first came across this concept when reading a book called *Anatomy of the Spirit*, by Caroline Myss. This book changed my perception of nursing and how to care for patients. These days I have a tendency to point out the secondary gain that I feel is keeping people from wanting to deal with their illness. However, I was not always aware of the bigger picture. You can guarantee that whenever someone has a recurrent problem, there is always an element of secondary gain. Whether this is the friend(s) who offer the sympathetic shoulder to cry on, the process of making up each time, the money from benefits or the excuse to not have to do something else, there is always an element of secondary gain.

Often these cycles are learned and may well be energetic programming playing out, as we discussed earlier. Whatever illness, problem, excuse, pain or challenge people are stuck in, they are usually getting some aspect of secondary gain. This is why victim support groups can be a double-edged sword. They provide support but only as long as you remain a victim. If you stopped being a victim then you would not need the support of the group. People bond and make friends in such environments, with the same thing in common – they are victims. If they were not, they would have no place at the group.

I am not saying that such groups do not play an important role in helping people through some challenging times. What I am saying is that maybe the process of guiding people out of the group, like a young bird leaving the nest, could be a little more effective and empowering in some cases.

Exercise: Flush out secondary gain.

Think of the area in your life that is currently providing you with your biggest challenge and ask yourself the following questions:

1: What is this problem preventing me from doing, which, if this problem disappeared I'll have to do?

2: What is it that I am doing, which I enjoy doing, which I won't be able to do if the problem disappears?

In the next chapter, we will take a look at how your everyday language can influence your life, heart and communications.

Chapter 10

How to Use Your Language to Get Better Results

A ccording to Oxford Dictionaries, there are over 250,000 words in the English language. The figure is reported to be over 1 million words by the Global Language Monitor. Yet, according to Answers.com the average person only uses between 1,500–2,000 words in their daily language.

There is a vast array of words to describe how you feel, what you want and explain any situation in the most minute detail. A creative linguist has the power to influence and sublimely dazzle others with their in-depth knowledge of the English language.

Whilst being aware of a wider array of linguistic options can be a wonderful thing, there are certain principles that need to be acknowledged, in order for you to optimise your communication outcomes. For anyone not familiar with the field of Neuro-Linguistic Programming (NLP) then I shall offer you perhaps the most important principle:

The human brain cannot process a negative.

You may well be wondering what that means in practical terms, so allow me to explain. If I tell you not to think about what you ate for breakfast today, are you able to do it? Or did you just think about what you ate for breakfast today? Maybe you skipped breakfast, but don't think about that either. If I ask you not to read on under any circumstances, what are you left thinking about?

When my nephews were three and four years old, they were playing in my mum's garden. There are a series of paving slabs that run down the garden and they were busy jumping from one paving slab to the next, paying careful attention to staying on the slabs. My sister popped her head around the door and shouted, 'Stay off the grass you two.' I watched their heads turn and they started to smile.

Less than a minute later, they were sliding down the grass and my sister was left wondering why they did not listen to her instructions. The fact is that they did, the instructions were just communicated in a way that the human brain cannot process. It is possible that if she had said nothing, they would have never even thought about going on the grass. A better communication would have been, 'Stay on the paving slabs.' This way, she would have communicated exactly what she wanted them to do and not planted a suggestion of something that she didn't.

Bad publicity is relative.

As a teenager, I frequently felt myself drawn towards anything that I was told not to do. Films that I shouldn't watch, places that I shouldn't go to and things that I shouldn't do were frequently on my list of things to investigate. I may not have done half of the things that I did if I hadn't been told not to do them.

I would probably never have read Dan Brown's *Da Vinci Code* if I hadn't read a statement from the Vatican saying that it wasn't true. Activists, like Mary Whitehouse, were responsible for increased sales in pornography after being very vocal in telling people not to watch it. I used to wonder as a teenager what she was doing watching it if it was so bad.

There is an episode of *Father Ted* that puts this point across wonderfully. The two priests are told to stand outside the local cinema and protest about a film with an obscene amount of nudity in it. As they stand outside the cinema with their placards reading, 'Down with that sort of thing,' local residents ask them questions about how bad it is, before walking into the cinema.

If you want people to do something, then tell them what you want them to do, not what you don't.

If I ask you not to *forget* this lesson, that may appear the same as *remember* this lesson, but it is communicating the complete opposite message to the human brain. If I tell you not to *leave the lid off* the marmalade, it is a very different thing than me telling you to *put the lid back on* the marmalade.

So, if someone asks you how you are today and you respond 'Not too *bad*,' you are actually communicating that you are bad. Using not and bad in the same sentence is a double negative. Is this really what you want to be putting out there? I use this example because I come across it so regularly in the UK. It is one step down from 'OK,' 'Alright' and 'So, so.'

Say something different.

What if the next time someone was to ask you how you were, you responded, 'Fantastic,' 'Wonderful' or 'Incredible'? It is quite possible that by becoming aware of your language and using these terms more regularly, you can change the results that you get in your life. You may not feel fantastic and want to be honest about how you feel. In that case, saying something like 'I've felt *better*,' 'not too *good*' or 'not exactly *brilliant*,' are better statements for your body and mind to process.

Ask better questions to get better results.

When you ask people questions, do you phrase them *positively*, or not? As a nurse I used to ask my patients questions like, 'Are you still *in pain?*' 'Did you have a *bad night?*' or 'Are you still *feeling sick?*' After learning about NLP, I started re-evaluating the questions that I asked my patients. I then chose to ask more empowering questions like, 'Are you *feeling better* yet?' 'Did you *sleep well?*' or 'Can you *feel any improvement* yet?'

Whilst none of these questions on their own will guarantee a more favourable outcome, they are conveying a much more positive message to those that you ask. This is a fascinating area and I encourage you to investigate the field of NLP further if this foundation has interested you. Personally, I have found NLP to be an excellent resource, which has greatly shifted my ability as a healer, trainer and communicator.

A phrase that I had been using as a nurse for years suddenly became apparent. 'Are you in any pain today?' I had been asking this of—all patients who had been experiencing pain as a course of habit. More often than not they would tell me that they did and required painkillers. I changed this question to 'Are you feeling better yet?' The results were incredible, especially when I asked it with a smile. Patients started saying yes way more often. I saved the National Health Service a lot of money in analgesia use when I started adopting my language towards positive outcomes.

> *Exercise: Write down at least three phrases that you use regularly, which could be improved in light of what we have discussed. Then write down a phrase for each one of them that could communicate your message in a more empowering and effective way.*

In the next chapter, we will look at why believing in your convictions is essential for the health of your heart.

Chapter 11

Believe in Yourself, Regardless of What Anyone Else Says

W e could talk about this subject all day and still only scratch the surface. You may already believe more in yourself since the beginning of this book, or you may not. Though the odds are that if you've read this far you probably have some work to do. This journey is ongoing.

Either way, we are going to take a look at why this aspect of wellbeing is at the heart of your self-destruct button and is the most important aspect of all. Ultimately, this is the first branch out of the root of your health and wellbeing, which stems from your ability to love yourself unconditionally.

Great leaders are great leaders because they think and do things differently.

We have looked at this earlier and now we will take it further. If you are going to be true to yourself, true to your heart and in alignment with your true purpose then there may well come a time when you must go against the opinion of the majority. Indeed, this could even involve going against the opinion of everyone that you know.

Your need to fit in, be liked and find connection can often lead to unhealthy compromise and can affect your mental health adversely if taken too far. It is this drive that sees young gang members coerced into crime. It is also the reason why people are likely to 'turn a blind eye' at work to certain things and practices, when everyone else around them does the same.

The desire to fit in and not to rock the boat can be very powerful and also very damaging to your overall health. Everyone who initiated huge changes in history would have to have first broken free of the accepted tribal beliefs that were in place beforehand.

Ruby Bridges was just six years of age in 1960, when she became one of the first black girls to attend a previously all white school. She had to be escorted to and from school each day to protect her from the angry parents of the white children. As parents of the white children pulled their children out of Ruby's class, she was forced to continue learning on a different floor to all of the other children for the rest of the year.

It took many years for Ruby to see the benefits in what she did but in 1995 her story was published, Disney made a movie about her and she was reunited with her old teacher on The Oprah Winfrey Show. It may not have been Ruby's decision to break such a barrier but her mother's belief that things needed to be better for her child made her take a step which would go on to inspire others and break boundaries that many would have never thought possible at the time.

Standing by your beliefs could even save your life.

My grandad rarely spoke about his role during the war and had reservations about some of the things that he was asked to do. However, this was out of his hands and on the rare occasion that he did talk about it, I would listen to his every word. The world that he grew up in was a very different place to the one that I had been exposed to.

He was a navigator in Bomber Command. During the Second World War, he did not have much money living in Belfast and felt that joining Fighter Command, as a pilot, was the way forward. His refusal to accept what he felt was unfair treatment during his training in the USA was enough to see him miss out on getting a commission. Indeed, his instructor even refused to instruct him and he had to learn how to fly a plane by listening to one of the other trainee pilots and taking the plane out on his own. Because the selection process involved only accepting three out of every group of six, he was never likely to be chosen amongst the three of a trainer who refused to train him.

Consequently, he went to Canada, to learn how to be a pilot there. After a few months, the Base Commander issued an instruction that everyone was to buy their own cutlery, at 50 cents each. Because a large amount of cutlery had gone missing from the canteen, this was deemed a necessary action.

He took decisive action.

My grandad was sending money back to my granny each week, leaving him little left of his own. Consequently, he refused to pay the 50 cents for his cutlery. There were a few thousand men in the base and he was the only one who refused. There was a group of Australian airmen who dissented initially but they relented after a while. This left my grandad to take the full force of the Commanding Officer, yet he still stood by his convictions.

He was then stripped of his place in Fighter Command and his status as a pilot. His only option within the system was to join Bomber Command as a navigator, where he remained for the next two years. It was only a chance meeting with a journalist that unearthed the fact that my grandad had been given a commission 18 months earlier, but he had not been told about it. Clearly, the Canadian command had not deemed it important enough to tell him that he was ready to serve in the war. Was this down to the fact that he had stood by his beliefs and ruffled a few feathers by doing it? Possibly.

Retaliation can be hazardous.

My grandad's first mission was a night bombing raid over Berlin. His bomber was bigger, slower and less well armed than the fighters that came to shoot it down. Because every third bullet was a tracer bullet and lit up whenever they fired their machine guns, it gave away their position. This attracted fire from the German fighters.

My grandad's crew concluded after that experience that it was not a good idea to use their machine guns and they never did again. Bomber Command took the highest losses of any Allied unit in the Second World War. They lost an average of 7% of their personnel on every raid they went on. Statistically, you should be dead for every 13 missions that you fly. Bomber Command told my grandad that they would release him if he was still alive after 28 missions.

Beating the odds.

During one raid my grandad's plane was fired upon six times by German fighters, almost completely ripping off one of the wings, yet he still made it back. For this he was awarded the Distinguished Flying Cross. After his 28 missions, the shortage of men meant that he was asked to continue. He went on to complete 36 missions over Germany, making him statistically dead three times. Meanwhile, his brother was shot down and killed over The Bay of Biscay.

He was more than lucky to be alive during the time he served. Had he agreed to purchase his cutlery three years earlier in the Canadian air base it could have also seen him being on the front 18 months earlier. This could have quite probably cost him his life. His example has stayed with me as a strong reminder that it is sometimes not only necessary to stand your ground and believe in yourself, but it could also be the difference between life or death.

Luck comes in many different shapes and forms.

Interestingly, one of the closest calls that my grandad had was not in the air. He returned from a bombing mission one morning and it was usual for him to go to the Bomber Command Mess Hall. This was something that he did immediately after landing after almost every mission. I say almost because on one occasion he was met by his Commanding Officer and taken into his office for a debrief.

It was a foggy morning and pilots were told to follow the instructions of the radio operator. On this occasion one of the landing pilots did not do this, confusing the lights of the Bomber Command Mess Hall with the runway, and crashed, taking out the entire Mess Hall. If Grandad had not been called in for the debrief he would have been dead with several other bomber crewmen.

How do you access more self-belief?

As we have already discussed, it is important to know your motivation strategy. When you know this then picture how you think your life will be in five years time if nothing changes. You will be older and possibly less healthy, less active, less vibrant and less happy. If you sit with this image and the feeling associated with it, then it may just trigger your pain strategy into taking decisive action now. You can aid this process by watching the film or reading the book *A Christmas Carol* by Charles Dickens. This book captures the essence of how to turn up the pain enough to cause action. If you are pleasure-motivated then just imagine how you will feel when you achieve your big, audacious goal.

Sometimes, pain will present itself, forcing you to act in accordance with your heart.

When I returned from Thailand in 2006, I joined a nursing agency. I had left nursing because I knew that it did not feel right for me, yet I had returned to nursing as it was the most convenient way that I knew to earn money. I had taken a step backwards but I had convinced myself that it would not be for long. Because I had adopted a 'moving away from' strategy of not having any money, I was quick to forget why I had left nursing in the first place.

Have you ever slipped back into a habit, job or relationship that you knew would not work for you?

This is very common. The paradox of life is that the human spirit craves both certainty and uncertainty. You may love knowing that regular money is arriving into your bank account, yet hate your job. You may love being in a relationship, yet hate the person you are with. You may love the idea of giving up everything and changing your life completely, yet hate the uncertainty and fear that it could bring. For me, I loved having money to travel and enjoy my life but I hated nursing. It wasn't the job or the patients, but the poor management decisions based on sometimes ridiculous government initiatives to make the service more efficient. Placing efficiency directives on a care service has sometimes fatal consequences for patients on the front line and I wasn't one to keep quiet about such things.

However, in my mind I was not free enough to believe that I could earn more in another line of work. If you have ever returned to something or someone, knowing that there would be pain involved, then you know what I mean. If you don't, then well done.

Extreme pain is often necessary to hammer home lessons that we refuse to accept.

There were numerous small incidents and difficult staff members that I had to negotiate during this eight-month period where I became a nurse again. However, it was not until I accepted a job that meant commuting to someone's house that things changed. I was introduced to a family who had four children, two of whom had a rare, progressively degenerative disease. It was difficult to diagnose and had caused the family plenty of pain, as doctors continually failed to diagnose it.

The prognosis for this disease was that if you lived to age seven, you were lucky. The eldest of the two sons who had the disease was sent home when he was about five with a care package, to die. Through love, belief and unwavering commitment both boys were still alive over 13 years later, defying all of the medical research available. They were the most inspirational family that I had ever met and taught me more about faith and the power of positive thinking than any teacher.

During my night shifts at the house, my job was to keep the oldest boy comfortable, change him and suction him occasionally. His condition meant that he was fed through a tube in his stomach and constantly producing mucus, which could have killed him if it wasn't suctioned out. I had been thinking about leaving nursing for a long time, and I had even left it for over three years, only to return. I kept ignoring my feelings about my nursing career, with judgements about how this was the fastest way for me to earn money.

One night I became complacent.

One night I had brought in a new laptop and found myself distracted. I had noticed that the suction was not working quite as efficiently as it did usually and forgot to tell the nurse I handed over to. In a hospital setting, this would be poor practice but would not have been an issue, as we had replacements at hand. In a home-care setting, this was a potentially lethal mistake. It led to me being asked not to come back by the family.

This incident hurt me on many levels.

My immediate pain was the fact that I was guilty of gross negligence, which could have led to the death of someone vulnerable. This was compounded by the fact that I had taken time to get to know the family and they were all incredible, inspirational individuals from whom I had learned much. I had let them all down.

Also, they could have reported me for negligence and endangering the life of their son, which could have led to a tribunal, stress, humiliation and potentially having my nursing registration revoked. Despite me endangering the life of their son, they did not report me to the agency or nursing council. They said only that they did not wish for me to work in their house again.

Being the pain-motivated person that I am, this had sent me over my threshold.

I knew in my mind that I could have been struck off the nursing register over this. However, it was the fact that I had rewarded a family, who had made me feel so welcome, taught me so much and been so good to me, by endangering the life of their son/brother. In my mind, this was enough for me to take matters into my own hands. I decided at that moment to strike myself off the nursing register. I would never work as a nurse again.

I sacked myself.

I was too embarrassed to tell many people what had really happened at the time and extremely disappointed with myself, after setting such a high benchmark for patient care during my career on the wards. By the standards that I had set myself, this was an unforgivable slip and a clear sign that it was time to move on and take a leap of faith. Finally, I had triggered my pain-motivation action strategy. Had I remembered and owned the reasons that I had left nursing back in 2003 then this would never had been necessary. What had been missing was the self-belief that I was ready to make it in the world of business.

If you are currently unhappy with any aspect of your life then your pain threshold will be continually tested, in increasingly distressful ways, until your head gets the message of your heart. From here, you need to start believing in yourself and the power that you have when your head and heart align.

Who do you believe in the most?

Think of the person who you believe in the most. What do they have that you don't yet? We are not just talking about self-belief here. What is their motivation? What is driving them to do what they do every day? Who do they surround themselves with? What would you need more of in your life in order to believe more in what you are doing? Who are you spending your time with, that is not serving you to achieve what you want? What are you saying yes to, that you would be better off saying no to?

These are just a few questions to start you off. However, it is only through connecting to your purpose, your vision and your intended legacy that you will access more self-belief. When you have a purpose that fills your heart with joy and start inspiring other people, then you will attract people and things into your life that support you and help you to stay on your path, even on those days where things do not appear that easy.

You have the world at your fingertips.

With the power of the internet and social networks such as Facebook and Twitter, it is now easier to connect with the rest of the world than it has ever been. You can find out how to do almost anything on YouTube, just by typing in what you are looking for. There are resources to create your own internet space or website for free and build up a following of people.

With just one click of a button, you can broadcast your message to others from all over the world, connecting in an instant. There is a world of opportunity at your fingertips just waiting for you to use it to your advantage.

Balance all thinking with action.

Because you learn by association, why not include a daily planning walk into your routine? Take at least five minutes to leave your desk and go for a walk each day. During this period, decide at least one positive action that you will take, and then return, write it down, and do it. Tiny steps now can lead you to incredible possibilities.

The secret behind *The Secret*.

If you have read *The Secret* by Rhonda Byrne or anything else to do with the law of attraction and are reading this wondering why the wonderful things that you have been attempting to manifest have not fallen in your lap yet, there is something else. It is not just about thinking of something and then waiting for it to come your way; you have to feel it. Until you manage to imagine that you already have what you are after and *feel* as though you would if you already had it, then it will not come to you.

Manifestation is not an intellectual process. If you have been looking to manifest things and have not been successful then you probably already know this. Knowing what you want is a good starting point. Feeling as though you already have it is the thing that will start to draw things towards you. Manifesting with your head alone will not work. Manifestation is a heart-based exercise.

Know why you want what you want.

So many people I know who have wanted to manifest things focus on getting a large sum of money. When I ask them why they want that specific amount, they don't really know. Often it is so that they do not have to work again ('away-from' motivation). The amount is usually a figure they have just plucked out of the air at random and they have no idea exactly how they would spend all of it, who else it would benefit or what greater purpose it would serve. It is just a thought, which is devoid of any real feeling, structure or belief.

The difference between 'I want a million pounds because I just do,' and 'I want a million pounds to buy land that can reforest part of The Amazon,' is a world apart. Having a vision to continually connect to, which stimulates you to feel more connected, more passionate and more alive, is essential if you are to increase your chances of manifesting exactly what you want.

When your 'why' is big enough the 'how' will take care of itself.

If you spend your time intellectualising about how you will achieve something, especially if it is a big, audacious goal, then you will probably get stuck. Focusing on the how before knowing your reason why will almost certainly tee you up for a harsh lesson or two. When you focus on the why, access the feeling and believe in yourself, you are opening your world up to things being drawn into your life, as if by magic. This is because your energy field is magnetic and your energy follows your thoughts.

You cannot possibly know what serendipitous events will unfold to connect you with your goal when you are feeling good about it on a regular basis. It is this feeling that is your key to attracting what you want into your life. When you are not feeling your goal, you are not attracting it.

Also know that if a goal is not in alignment with your purpose on this planet, it doesn't matter how much manifesting you do: it's unlikely to happen. This is very much a trial and error process.

Exercise: Think about your vision until you start to feel what it would be like if you already had it. Notice what changes happen in your mind and hold this feeling for at least two minutes. Repeat this regularly (at least every day). If your self-belief needs a little work then contemplate the question 'Why not me?' and write down anything that comes up.

In the next chapter, we will look at how everything has a reason.

Chapter 12

Chaos + Time = Understanding

So often incidents will happen in your life that appear chaotic, unfair, difficult or unjustified. These are the moments that have the potential to derail you or turn your life around. The only question is: will you have enough faith and self-belief to persist until the bigger picture reveals itself?

Some things can just appear so wrong.

In the summer of 2010, I returned to my home to find that someone had smashed my back door, leaving it in hundreds of pieces. Broken glass and wood were strewn across the carpet. I went upstairs to find that someone had been through my bedside drawers containing all of my most personal and valuable contents. They had been emptied out on my bed.

My initial reaction was one of shock. St Albans is not known for this sort of thing. I had heard of friends who had been burgled but it is one of those things that, until it has happened to you, you will never really be able to fully comprehend it. It was not the broken door, the stolen money or the inconvenience that gave me the biggest food for thought, it was the fact that they had been going through my most personal items: my notes, my gifts and letters that I had received. I phoned my sister and my dad to ask if they knew anyone who could help.

Then the other side of the coin began to show itself to me.

My dad was able to find someone to help, as did my sister. At 9pm, this was no mean feat. I had to ask one of them not to come. It had been raining in London when I left there but, fortunately, it was not raining in St Albans. If it had been I would have had a house filled with rain. I also met my neighbours, who did not hear anything but were very helpful. Incredibly, I had not met many of them before this incident.

The robbers had left everything alone in my front room, leaving it for me exactly how I had left it. I had some valuable equipment in there which wasn't taken. I had an envelope with all of my remaining cash in the drawer below the one that was emptied (over £1,000, which was not taken). Instead, the contents of an envelope I had kept were strewn over my bed. This contained notes of gratitude from my friends, which I had kept but not read for over a year.

Had the burglars looked for a little longer they would have found most of the money that I owned in the world at that time, leaving me with less than £100 in the bank. Of course, the question arises as to why I had so much cash in my bedroom and so little in the bank. I had always kept £1,000 cash in my bedroom as an emergency fund. Strangely enough, I no longer do this. It had been kept in the bottom drawer in my bedside cabinet. All other drawers had been opened and emptied but they had inexplicably left that one undisturbed.

In reading my gratitude notes, the burglars had not even taken all of the money from that drawer. Some more cynical friends were sure that it was because the burglars were disturbed. Maybe they had lost valuable time in reading my notes of gratitude, when they were so close to taking almost everything that I owned.

I sat on my bed reading through my gratitude notes.

Each one was from a different friend met during a training course that I had been on. We were encouraged to write notes of gratitude about how our lives had been affected by each other. Some of the notes were so deep and heartfelt that my eyes filled up with tears of gratitude. I had been struggling with my life and business for over a year, whilst ignoring such a powerful resource that had been next to my bed. It had taken a burglar to remind me of this.

Many people have speculated as to what happened to the burglars after breaking into my house. They were clearly guided to go to my bedroom, and that of my housemate. They broke the door, stole a sat-nav from my housemate and about £100 from me. Otherwise, they left everything intact. I would like to think that they were at least a little bit moved after reading my gratitude notes. I guess I will never know for sure.

The positives of the situation unfolded over time.

A man arrived to patch up the door that evening, making the house safe from the elements. I met three neighbours that I had never spoken to before, all of whom were eager to do what they could for me. Communities are often brought closer during times of adversity. I read through all of my gratitude notes, feeling further gratitude for the equipment and money that wasn't taken. I then wrote about this experience and posted it on Facebook, tagging all of my friends who had written me the notes of gratitude. It was by far the most popular post I had put on there, attracting numerous comments from some wonderful people.

The house owner had the door fixed quickly enough and my dad gave me the same amount of money that I had stolen from me. All in all, it was one of the best things that happened to me that year. Had I evaluated the incident from the thoughts that crossed my mind when I entered the house then I would have surely experienced a much bleaker outlook than I actually did. It also opened me up to receiving, something that I had not been great at until that point in time. It was a very moving and deeply humbling experience.

Evaluating chaos as it happens will rarely present you with the bigger picture, which is always at play.

Because of a number of factors, some of which we have addressed in this book, it often takes a shock to trigger a change that can change perspective. There is the phrase that hindsight is 20/20. It is much easier to look over incidents from the past and assess them more objectively than it is to do as they arise. Sometimes, even the most disastrous situations can yield positives over time.

Surely being around for a nuclear attack can never be a good thing?

Tsutomu Yamaguchi happened to be in Hiroshima, on business, when the nuclear strike occurred on 6 August 1945. Despite going deaf in his left ear and sustaining some other injuries, he headed back to his hometown of Nagasaki, returning to work on 9 August, just in time for the second nuclear strike.

Not only did Mr Yamaguchi survive both blasts, he went on to speak out against nuclear weapons, inspiring and influencing people until his death in 2010. Had he assessed his situation in the hours after either nuclear strike, it is unlikely that he would have been seeing many positives.

This can also happen in reverse.

I could use the Trojan horse as my example but that may or may not have happened. One thing that really did happen was that Jack Whittaker woke up on Christmas Day 2002 to find out that he had just won $315 million on the powerball lottery. He was, of course, a happy man upon finding out this news.

He was then besieged by requests for help and gave out $50 million in gifts and donations. Suddenly he had become the people's Santa Claus. From this point onwards, things started to change for him. Four hundred lawsuits were made against him or one of his companies, costing him $3 million in legal bills alone. He began drinking heavily, becoming friendless and lonely.

Perhaps the biggest blow for Mr Whittaker was what happened to his granddaughter, Brandi, whom he was very close to. He showered her with money and gifts. This led her to taking illegal drugs and two years later, she was found dead, wrapped in a plastic sheet and dumped. This devastated Mr Whittaker and made him feel that he had been cursed. Unfortunately, this is one of many tragic stories of lottery winners who did not do so well afterwards.

What about you?

How many times in your life has a situation that appeared terrible at the time yielded positive outcomes later? Conversely, how often has something seemingly wonderful proved to be not so good down the line?

Evaluating people, things and situations as they appear at first is a largely pointless activity. Unless you are gifted with particularly sharp and well-developed instincts or incredible psychic skills then it is unlikely that sifting through the presenting facts in many of life's challenging situations will yield much sense. It is only trust, belief and the ability to let go of judgement that will truly guide you through such testing times.

> *Exercise: List three events in your life that appeared really bad at the time, yet proved to yield unexpected gifts down the line. Feel free to use events that you feel have not yet yielded anything positive, and consider what you learned of value from them.*

There is one other crucial element to this, which we will explore in the next chapter.

Chapter 13

The Cultivation of Luck

Are you feeling lucky?

I was tempted to add 'punk' on the end of that statement, as I chuckle away to myself. The image of Clint Eastwood's *Dirty Harry* is an iconic image when I think about luck. Assuming that you have not been in the position of having a gun pulled on you or had a swift game of Russian roulette, then luck probably means something very different to you. My dad has always believed that he was lucky and encouraged me to consider myself lucky. This is something that has been a great benefit to me throughout my life.

Napoleon once stated: 'Give me lucky Generals.' He believed that this was the most important quality for his men to have. Ironically, Napoleon is probably most famously remembered in the UK for losing the battle of Waterloo, yet he won more battles than Caesar, Alexander the Great and Frederick the Great put together.

The Oxford Dictionary describes luck as, 'success or failure apparently brought on by chance rather than through one's own actions'. This would be a common belief about luck. However, there has been much study on this subject and it has been proven that you can improve your tendency towards being lucky. There are plenty of people who say things like 'You make your own luck,' or 'It's not luck, it's hard work.' There are elements of truth in these statements; you certainly can make your own luck and there is some work involved but you can influence how lucky you are.

Research on luck.

Professor Richard Wiseman conducted a study on luck. He placed an advert asking people who thought that they were really lucky or unlucky to contact him. He then handed them a newspaper and asked them to go through it and tell him how many photographs were inside. Halfway through the paper he had printed an advert, taking over half a page, in big, two-inch letters, 'Tell the experimenter that you have seen this and win £250.'

He found that the unlucky people tended to miss it, whilst the lucky people tended to spot it. Unlucky people were found to be more tense, which led to them missing opportunities, as they were busy focusing on something else. Lucky people tend to be more relaxed and open, allowing them to see opportunities, rather than just what they are looking for.

Even a crisis can prove lucky.

On one trip, back in May 1998, from London to Perth, I would find out exactly how lucky I was. As I was travelling on a budget, my flight involved stopovers at Frankfurt, Abu Dhabi, Jakarta and Bali. I was used to such long-haul flights so I expected this to be just another routine journey. At Jakarta, I found myself distracted and lost in the airport. Consequently, I missed my connecting flight. This is a very rare thing for me. However, I decided to go to the airport desk and see if I could get on the next flight.

Chaos awaited me.

It became clear at the desk that something was very wrong indeed. The person allocating the tickets was confused as reports came in that all further flights had been cancelled indefinitely. Passengers surrounded him like a pack of animals, many screaming demands at him. I stood at the back and started talking to a lovely girl from New Zealand. After chatting for a while she told me that she was travelling with three others and that they were sitting at the cafe waiting for her. It also turned out that they were going to Bali too.

We agreed that it would be nice to travel together and I took all of our tickets to the man at the desk. As other tourists screamed at him, I pulled him aside and told him that I knew that he did not know what was going on at the moment but would be grateful if when he did, he would put all of us on the next flight to Bali. He appeared grateful that I was being so reasonable and took the tickets.

I then joined my new friends for a drink or two in the airport.

After 12 hours, I was very drunk, having fun with my new friends and eyeing up a place to sleep on the airport floor. I had even decided to change my itinerary and stay in Bali for a couple of weeks. As government warnings were encouraging people to leave Indonesia quickly, there was a long queue of people wanting to change their flights. When I told the man at the desk that I wanted to extend my stay, he looked at me as if I were mad. He questioned my decision and I assured him that I was certain. I had little idea of how events were unfolding.

I also decided to phone home to tell my parents how much fun that I was having. It appears that the news broadcasts of riots in Jakarta had made it home. This phone call did not go down well with my parents, as they thought that my life might be in danger. Unfortunately, I was too drunk to remember exactly what I said to them at the time but I did laugh a lot.

Before I could finish my call it was announced that we were on the next flight out, which was departing immediately. I had to hang up and run for the boarding gate. I had not realised at the time how my parents must have been feeling about me being in a rioting city and having to hang up and run quickly. They were less than happy it took me over two weeks to call them again.

We caught the flight to Bali, met two more girls who joined us on our trip, and stayed in Bali for a few days. In the paper, the next day was the headline '499 people killed in Jakarta riots.' I was shocked. Tourists were leaving Bali in droves and the currency went into free-fall. My money was suddenly worth four times what it had been worth on my previous visit, one month earlier.

From a riot to paradise.

The group of us moved from Bali after a few days to a lovely island on the north, east of Bali, called Gili Air. It was a very small island that I could walk around in 45 minutes. I stayed in a beautiful beach hut on an empty, idyllic beach with my new friends. It cost me about £1 per day. A further £1 would be charged for a three-course meal and 50p to hire snorkels and masks for the day to see the beautiful clear waters off the beach. The country may have been in chaos but I was in paradise.

I felt very lucky indeed.

I made friends with numerous locals, some of whom took us on their boat for the day. We provided the booze and they provided the cruise. That evening we discovered what phosphorescence was. As we dived into the sea at night, it would light up, like a scene from *Fantasia*.

During that trip I spent two weeks and next to nothing in an island paradise, met some great people, had the best island holiday ever and spent many hours on my hammock overlooking the crystal clear waters, contemplating how lucky I was.

Luck comes in many forms.

On 1 March 1950 at West Side Baptist Church in Beatrice, Nebraska, choir practice was due to start at 19.20 as usual that evening. At 19.25, an explosion demolished the church, forcing the nearby radio station off air and shattering several windows of nearby homes. Fortunately, the 15-strong choir all turned up late for practice that day, thus surviving the blast.

In 1989, a Philadelphia financial analyst discovered something in an old picture he'd bought for $4 at a flea market. He wanted it only for the frame but found an old copy of the Declaration of Independence between the canvas and the wood backing. Not only did he sell it for $2.42 million dollars, but it was resold in June 2000 for $8.14 million dollars.

Robert Cunningham, a 30-year police veteran, offered Phyllis Penzo, a waitress at Sal's Pizzeria, a half share of his lottery ticket as a tip. The next day, true to his word, he returned to give her $3 million dollars, her half share of the prize. Was Phyllis lucky?

Frane Selak. Possibly the luckiest person to have lived.

Frane Selak, a Croatian music teacher, has had more than his fair share of luck, or bad luck, depending how you see it. During his lifetime, he has managed to escape from a derailed train, a door-less plane, a bus crash, a flaming car and two other car accidents. He then went on to win $1 million on the lottery.

Some of these incidents were particularly incredible. In 1962, Mr Selak was on a train from Sarajevo to Dubrovnik. When the train derailed and plunged into an icy river 17 people died. Mr Selak escaped with just a broken arm. During a flight in 1963 from Zagreb to Rijeka, a door blew off, forcing him out of the plane in mid-air. He miraculously landed in a haystack, suffering only minor injuries, but 19 others died in the crash.

In 1966, his bus fell into a river, killing four people. Again, Mr Selak escaped unharmed. In 1970, he managed to escape before a faulty fuel pump engulfed his car in flames. In 1973, he had a shock when fire started shooting through the air vents of his car. Despite the loss of most of his hair, he came out unharmed. In 1995, he was hit by a bus and, once again, escaped unharmed.

In 1996, he was forced to drive his car off a cliff to escape an oncoming truck. He fell out of the car and landed in a tree and watched as his car exploded below him. In 2003 he won $1 million in the Croatian lottery and said, 'I know God was watching me over all these years.' He also said that he could be considered 'the world's unluckiest man or the world's luckiest man.' He prefers the latter, though I'm not sure I'd be ready to go travelling with him!

Believe in luck.

Frane's example is an extreme one. However, if your life unfolded in the same way as his, would you consider yourself lucky or not? Often I hear lucky people tell me that they believe that someone is watching over them. Whether this is true or not, it clearly works. Believing in luck and feeling lucky are very good for your heart.

There are ways for you to become luckier.

Professor Wiseman's study found four ways to increase the luck of all of the subjects. Consider this your next exercise:

> *Trust your gut instincts as they are normally right.*
> *Be open to new experiences and breaking your normal routine.*
> *Spend a few moments each day remembering things that went well.*
> *Visualise yourself being lucky before an important meeting or telephone call.*
> *Luck is very often a self-fulfilling prophecy.*

Now it's time to plunge into the darker side of life and heart health, in our next chapter.

Chapter 14

The Dark Side of Your Heart

I t is all well and good wanting to live a spiritual life and pursuing all things pure, but this is simply not what life is all about. It is certainly not the only thing that your heart needs. By cutting off the darker aspects of life, you are cutting off your path to your heart's true message and your light within.

You have a dark side.

Your dark side is just as big a part of you as your lovely, spiritual, light side. I deliberately talk about the dark side, as the *Star Wars* films have been such a prominent feature in my journey on this path. The extremities of dark and light in these films provide a great contrast for what I am saying. When *Star Wars* was first at the cinema I was five years old. My dad took me to see it. I loved it. It scared me, entertained me and resonated deep within me. Much as I loved Yoda and Luke Skywalker, it was Darth Vader who made the biggest impression on me.

For those of you not old enough to remember, cinemas used to have a break halfway through the film. At this point people would enter the cinema, selling sweets and ice creams. Add chocolate and an array of sugary delights to a bunch of children and you get noise and activity in abundance. When the second half of the film started, the cinema was like a carnival. The next scene commenced with Darth Vader's cold, dark presence, silencing a cinema full of screaming kids, instantly. This is quite a talent considering we were all fuelled with sugar. Not really surprising that they stopped that practice!

I have watched all of the *Star Wars* films several times and always take away a new, spiritual teaching each time I watch one of them. When I compare the *Star Wars* movies to the entire spiritual, energetic and real-life learning experiences that I have had, I believe that they encapsulate the many complicated aspects of life that many of us struggle with at times.

Dark forces are always at work.

Whatever you make of the darker aspects of life, they will always come from within you. You only need to watch the news to find someone being killed, raped, mugged, abandoned, lied to, beaten or deceived. The world is filled with people doing these things. This is where judgements from your head can cut you off from the bigger picture at work here.

Guilt and judgement are at the root of all self-destruct buttons. You discover your dark side by listing the five things that you currently find absolutely inexcusable (extreme judgements). If there is nothing that you find absolutely inexcusable then you may not need to bother reading this section. At one stage in my life, I would have compiled a list something like: murder, rape, torture, treachery and theft.

It was always easy for me to sit in judgement of anyone who fell into any of these categories.

Should a murderer be murdered? Should a rapist be raped? Should a torturer be tortured? By judging these things to always be wrong and thinking that they should all be punished, a paradox is created in your life. Do you think these things are so wrong that they should be served as punishment to those that do them? If you do, like a large percentage of the population, then your dark side is starting to show. You may not be actually prepared to do these things yourself. If, however, you would agree to them being done to certain people then this is virtually the same thing. This type of 'an eye for an eye' approach just makes everyone blind.

Furthermore, there are a set of circumstances that could lead all of us to do terrible things. If, for example, you could only save a loved one by killing someone else, would you do it? Quite likely!

My path to the dark side.

I used to spend time as a child connecting with the cows in our field behind us. I would go up and stroke their heads and give them handfuls of grass and usher the flies away from their eyes. It was many years before I realised that they were being killed to provide me with my Sunday lunch. This conflict ran within me until I was 26 years old and became a vegetarian. I was prepared for cows to die in order for me to eat. This never felt right in my heart, yet I continued eating meat after finding this out for well over a decade before doing anything about it. Such inner conflict and the delay between wanting and doing are not good for mental health.

Killing animals may be part of life but it never felt right for me, so eventually I stopped eating meat. However, I knowingly accepted that killing would occur in order for me to eat. Allied with the ants that I used to pour boiling water over as a child and the many bugs that I killed, I was not making a very strong case for someone who judged killing as a terrible thing. For the record, I make no judgements towards anyone who eats meat. If you eat meat and it feels right for you, then it is right. I believe that vegetarians who judge meat-eaters are in more danger of heart disease than meat-eaters who just get on with their lives and feel good about what they eat.

The day that my dark side came out to play.

When I was 19 years old, I left England to work in an American Summer Camp. It was the first time ever that I had been away, travelling on my own. I had just handed in my notice at the merchant bank where I had been working for the past two years. I had been going slowly stir crazy, realising that a life of banking would have led me straight back to the lunatic asylum. I had been bored senseless by my role there and took a defiant step in handing in my notice. This did not please my family but it did please me.

I soon made friends with my new international and American co-workers, forming strong friendships very quickly. The excitement and adventure of being away and not knowing what was in store for me was a very liberating sensation. In the beautiful setting of the Pocono Mountains, in Pennsylvania, we were based in a stunning natural environment. There was a wonderful walk to a waterfall about two miles from the camp, where we would go with the kids every now and again.

One of the staff, a lifeguard at the swimming pool, was always friendly and talkative to me. We would share stories of our lives as the kids swam each day. She was always very warm, friendly and unassuming. She was a beautiful girl, with a beautiful soul.

A very dark day at the office.

After about 5 weeks of camp that summer, she went walking to the waterfall on her own. It was her day off. I returned from my day off to find out that she had been raped and shot in the head at the waterfall.

Panic swept the camp, parents were arriving to get their children out, reporters crowded the gates and police arrived to interview us all. Everyone on the camp was interviewed. I can honestly say that it felt more like an interrogation. At 19 years of age, I had not been prepared for anything like that. The less than friendly police officers left me feeling that they thought it was me who had done it.

I was shocked, angry, upset and more than slightly shaken by the incident. Counsellors were brought in and things were very odd for a few weeks afterwards. The staff certainly gelled in a way that was quite incredible. I am still in touch with some of the people that I met that summer.

This incident made me ask some dark questions.

Had I walked onto the scene as this incident happened, would I have been able to kill the perpetrator if it meant saving the life of my friend? I probably could have. If I'd found out that he had been sent to jail and was put in a cell surrounded by randy inmates, twice his size, would I have advocated his rape and torture? I most certainly would have. Would I be prepared to lie and deceive to have gained justice for this incident? For sure I would. Such a hateful and pointless killing of someone so radiant was way outside of anything logical in my head.

At the time, there was nothing that I would not have been prepared to sanction on the person who committed this act.

However justified my thoughts may appear to have been at the time, I was still prepared to advocate everything that I held to be totally unacceptable. Just one turn of fate was enough to turn my thoughts to the dark side and stand for everything that I had judged to be wrong. It was an area of my personality that I did not know existed, but it did. Just because I hadn't been put in a situation to realise it before, did not mean that it did not exist within me.

If you have never even thought about wanting someone dead or punished in extreme ways for a crime that they have committed then I congratulate you, you are probably enlightened and not reading this. But if you have ever even thought about wanting any of the things that you deem terrible, done to someone else, then you already know your dark side. Now it's time to embrace your darkness and realise that this is just as big a part of you as all of the goodness and love that you are capable of showing, regardless how justified you feel it is.

Shades of grey.

So many things in this world that appear irreconcilable will usually have a bigger picture, which you may never fully understand. Would there be as many criminals if everyone had model parents? Would there be as much killing if world leaders were not so fast to advocate wars or involve themselves in the affairs of other countries? If the lives of your loved ones were at stake, is there anything that you would not be prepared to do to save them?

The fact is that we all have a dark side.

Whilst I do not advocate that you dress up as Darth Vader, start breathing loudly and walk around spreading the dark side of the force, I am suggesting that you consider how you could react if someone that you loved was brutally killed. If you could forgive them easily and let go then well done. I'm guessing that you probably would not be able to do that straight away and that it is likely that you will at least entertain the notion of something less than pleasant happening to the murderer.

Only through embracing even the darkest aspects of human nature, letting go and forgiving, will you ever be able to access the lighter aspects of life. To do this it is necessary to realise that only freedom from judgement will enable you to access complete and vibrant health within your heart. Part of this is the area in your psyche that you think that you could not possibly share with anyone else. For whatever reason, you think that there are parts of you that would adversely affect the opinion of others. This is your dark side.

Too good to be true?

I realise that freedom from judgement will just remain a nice (or maybe not so nice) idea for you at the moment. You may spend your whole life learning this lesson, or not. However, if you make your goal accepting every aspect of yourself, your heart and your life, then you will constantly be edging towards a better place. It may not be easy. You will be tested. You will enter some very dark places. You will have to make some testing decisions and you will discover aspects of yourself that you didn't know that you had within you.

Exploring your dark side may not be as popular or appealing as discovering your healing abilities, magnificence and joy in life, but it is at least equally important. You cannot embrace one side of who you are fully, without embracing the other. Like Anakin Skywalker in *Star Wars*, we each can move

from one side of the force to the other. It is only your judgements about this
that cause the pain and disease within your heart.

You are capable of both wonderful and terrible acts.

If you are reading this and have never had at least one experience of acting in a
way that defies all logic, then congratulations, you may be a descendant of Mr
Spock. If you can recall at least one incident when you acted out of character,
then congratulations, you are a human being who is not yet enlightened. Most
of the population falls into this category.

Because you are both an emotional being and continuously fluctuating
between your dark and light aspects, there will always be incidents that trigger
you to react in ways that defy logic. Road rage is a classic example. Allowing
your head to pore over the facts and cast judgement on your heart is both
a foolish and dangerous act in regard to the health of your heart. You are
always acting in alignment with who you are. Just because you may not like
or approve of the darker aspects of your behaviour, does not mean that these
acts are not just as big a part of who you are as the times that you have acted
in a loving way.

Life's rollercoaster.

In life, your highs are only relative to your lows. Extreme joy and jubilation
is only ever relative to the hardest, darkest days where you had to lift yourself
off the ground, dust yourself down and keep going. If you achieved something
easily then it is likely that your appreciation is not quite on the same level as
it would have been if you had been severely tested, had to believe in yourself
and stay persistent.

Unconditional love sounds like a great ideal, yet this is not the experience
that most people have for most of the time. Life can deliver us all some very
testing and painful experiences. It is only the accumulation of such experiences
that makes the moments when your heart truly opens to love unconditionally,
so magical. For this reason, dark moments, dark acts and dark moods are just
as much a part of you receiving a truly rich experience of life than the joy,
jubilation and love that you get when you overcome challenges or encounter
moments so beautiful that they take your breath away.

Everyone loves to hate the villain.

Good films are only as good as the darkness of the villain. This is the essence of Hollywood and what makes an entertaining movie experience. Darth Vader is a prime example. Just remember that he not only started as a good guy, but his final act was to kill his evil master and save his son. Good and evil have a very fine line, as do your inner light and darkness. Not accepting this is the essence of lunacy for some. From a bigger picture, spiritual, point of view, it takes a noble soul to volunteer to play the role of the villain, to teach others qualities like strength and forgiveness.

Villains get to be judged and scorned by 'the light workers'.

Getting revenge or justice for atrocious acts is often the driving force of plots in films. The sense of justice that you may feel when the villain gets their comeuppance is a normal reaction from your logical, judgemental viewpoint. If you were to be truly one of the 'goodies' in life's movie you would never pass judgement on anyone else for anything. This is a big step towards a more enlightened life. If you are not yet enlightened then you can start by realising that every time you pass judgement on anyone else, then you disown a part of yourself. This creates separation, conflict within, pain and heart disease.

> *Exercise: Write down a list of things you have done which may have appeared out of character, perhaps events where you said something that you went on to regret, did something that you have never owned up to or acted in a way that shocked you afterwards. This is just as much a part of you as the lighter side of your nature. Ask yourself, what have I learned from all of these incidents and how did/could I balance them out?*

Now that we have explored the darker side of your heart, let us look at the incredible being within you that is capable of amazing things.

Chapter 15

The Incredible You

We have explored the darker nature of who you are so it is now only fair that we take a look at your potential. It is easy to set limitations on what you are capable of but you will never know what you can truly achieve until you are put into a situation where you have no time to think. During these times, you will discover aspects of yourself that you had no idea of and act in alignment with who you really are.

There are some things that you can speculate all you want about how you may react but you will never know unless you are placed in that situation. For example, if someone you didn't know pointed a loaded gun at your head, how would you react? Unless that has happened to you, you just don't know. It's likely to be different at different times as it will depend on your circumstances and ability to manage your mood and energy at the time.

I could quite easily dedicate an entire book to this section, highlighting incredible things, achieved by ordinary people, placed in extraordinary circumstances.

Tillie Tooter was 83 years old, when a hit and run driver forced her off a raised freeway in South Florida. She spent the next three days trapped on top of a mangrove tree, in her upside-down car, 40 feet below the road that she had been on. All she had with her was a cough drop, a peppermint and a stick of chewing gum. It was only that a passing landscaper noticed her car after three days that she was found and freed from her upside down position. She had been collecting rainwater in her quilted steering wheel cover and a pair of socks that she hung outside the window. If you had to do it, do you think you could?

In 1915, Wenseslao Moguel was sentenced to death by firing squad, without a trial, for his role as a soldier in the Mexican revolution. He was shot ten times, including once in the head, and left to die. He managed to wait for his executioners to leave before taking himself off to get help and recover. Could you defy death if you had to? You may never know.

Paul Templer was working as a guide along the Zambezi River. One day his tour was subjected to a surprise attack by a bull hippo, one of the most dangerous animals on the planet. His colleague was thrown into the water when his canoe was overturned. Mr Templer tried to save his colleague before finding himself lodged in the mouth of the hippo, with his head down its throat and his arms and body wedged between its teeth. He was then dragged underwater. Do you think you would have what it takes to pull yourself out of the mouth of a hippo, whilst you were underwater?

He somehow managed to free himself but was subjected to further frenzied attacks. During the assault Templer saw his foot ripped off, his arm severed, his ribs broken and holes torn into his back and chest. He emerged alive to have a six-hour operation, which included having his severed arm amputated, and then a very long recovery. He then returned to the river to continue working as a guide, a coach, public speaker and fundraiser for the children's charity 'Make-a-Difference'. Is Paul Templer superhuman or did he just discover that his heart was stronger than he could have possibly imagined?

Serious food for thought.

On Friday 13 October 1972, the Uruguayan Stella Marris rugby team were flying to a match in Chile when their plane crashed in the Andes. Many died in the crash, others died shortly after from injuries, and eight of them died in an avalanche after 17 days. Only 16 remained. They survived the extreme conditions by eating the flesh of their dead teammates. It was ten weeks after the crash when two of the team went on an expedition and found a passing Chilean horseman. Extreme situations require extreme measures. Would you eat human flesh to keep yourself alive? If your desire to live was strong enough you probably would.

What would you do?

On 24 December 1971, 17-year-old Juliane Koepcke was on a flight above the Peruvian rainforest, when her plane was hit by lightning. She was blown from the plane, still strapped to her seat, and landed two miles down in a dense thicket. When she came around, she was blind in one eye, with a broken collarbone, cuts and bruises. Everyone else on the plane had died. Wearing a mini-skirt and sandals, she trekked for nine days before finding a cabin to clean up her injuries and worm-infested cuts. She was eventually reunited with her father and continued her studies to become a zoologist. Could you have trekked for nine days with no supplies, let alone with one eye, a broken collarbone and infected cuts?

Where do you think your breaking point is?

John McCain spent five and a half years in the 'Hanoi Hilton' prison camp after being shot down on a bombing mission, where the North Vietnamese captured him. After nearly drowning in a lake, he was pulled from it by soldiers to have his shoulder crushed, and was bayoneted by his captors. He was then transported to his prison, beaten and tortured to the extent that he was not expected to live. McCain did live and was put in solitary confinement for two years. After a few months of solitary confinement, he was given the option of repatriation, due to his influential family ties. He could have gone home. He refused, unless all of the POWs that were captured before him were also released.

In August 1968, a programme of extreme torture was started on McCain. He was tied up and beaten every two hours as he suffered with dysentery. This led to a suicide attempt, which was stopped by guards. By the time that he was released, on 14 March 1973, his injuries were so great that he would never be able to lift his hands above his head again. Despite this, he went on to become an eminent figure in American politics.

Could you do the same?

You may be reading the above stories and thinking to yourself that you could never do that. John McCain went on to say that he was broken and that everyone has their breaking point. His suicide attempt proved this. The fact is that when your survival instinct kicks in then you will discover a side of yourself that you never knew you had. Heroes and heroines are ordinary people who are put in extraordinary situations, much like the people in the cases above. You may or may not discover this in your lifetime.

Incredible selflessness.

In August 2006, skydiving instructor Robert Cook was giving a skydiving lesson to a woman in Missouri, when it became apparent that the plane was going to crash. Believing that it was his duty to save Kimberly Dear, the girl that he had taken on board for the lesson, he hooked up her harness so that he would take most of the impact. When the plane crashed Robert and six others died, but his selfless act saved the life of Kimberly. Would you sacrifice your life for someone that you hardly knew?

Caught between a rock and a hard place.

Aron Ralston set out hiking in April 2003, in Blue John Canyon, Utah. When an 800-pound rock fell and crushed and trapped his forearm, things were looking particularly bleak for him, especially as he had not informed anyone that he was going hiking.

Assuming that he would die, he spent five days sipping the 350mls of water that he had, whilst attempting to free himself. The then delirious and dehydrated Mr Ralston managed to break his forearm and amputate the trapped arm with a small, cheap, pocketknife. Bleeding and dehydrated, he then managed to get down a 65-foot sheer wall and hike out of the canyon in the midday sun. Could you break your arm and cut it off with a small knife, climb and trek to safety if it meant staying alive? There is a movie about it called *127 hours*.

You never know when you will have to think quickly under pressure.

Whilst I have no personal experience that is anything close to the above situations, I have been faced with moments where I have been infused with acute panic and forced to draw on inner resources that I did not know existed. One such episode happened when I was playing on the trampoline with my nephews, Connor and Kian, who were four and three years old at the time.

This proved to be a fantastic way for them to have fun, keep fit and keep their boredom at bay. I also found that it was a great way for me to play with them.

Being typical three and four year olds, they had a very curious nature and liked to know everything. They have provided me with hours of entertainment and have been a real gift in my life. Experiencing the world through their eyes is a wonderful thing.

At a mind, body and spirit festival not long before this trampoline incident, I had purchased a pack of Angel cards. I wanted to show support for a friend with a stall there. I didn't really need anything that she was selling but decided that these cards might be a good gift for someone. The deck of cards had sat on my bedside cupboard, unopened, for a few weeks before my nephews found them.

'What are these, Uncle Ads?' My eldest nephew, Connor, asked me.

'They are Angel cards,' I replied

'What are they for?' Connor added.

'The Angels are there for us when we need help in our lives,' I told them.

'Can we play with the Angels?' my younger nephew, Kian, asked.

'Of course. But you need to tell them what you want help with.'

'I want more sweets. Can the Angels help me with that?' Kian asked.

'I think that you should ask your Mum for help with that. The Angels are for helping you with more important things,' I said, foolishly forgetting how important sweets are to them. I was also enjoying making up the story as I went along.

The two boys looked at me blankly for a few seconds before Connor added, 'Uncle Ads, I don't know what else to ask them.'

Our conversation continued until I guided them to a different goal. In this instance, they both asked the Angels for help with their school/nursery projects.

Each time they came around to the house after that they would rush up the stairs and ask the Angels for help with something. It became a central focus of their visits.

Shortly after their third consultation with the Angels, I was at my sister's house, playing with them on the trampoline. We played for well over half an hour and were all having a ball.

As excitement levels rose, we had an incident where I bounced on the trampoline causing Connor to fly up, with his feet directly above his head.

Time froze at that second as I helplessly watched him fall upon his head, causing his neck to jolt and him to scream out in pain as the trampoline jolted him a few more times. I was momentarily filled with terror – but I knew that I had to at least look as if I was calm and in control. Connor was screaming, hysterically. My first task was to tell my sister to call an ambulance. I repeated that everything was going to be OK and that he had amazing healing powers. I told him that he was feeling more relaxed and that he could ask for help from the Angels.

'Really Uncle Ads? Will the Angels help me?'

'If you ask them to.'

'Please help me Angels,' Connor asked, now visibly less distressed.

'Now that you have asked them – they are already helping you. Can you feel them help you?'

'Yes,' he smiled.

'Where are they helping you?'

'On my neck.'

'What colour is it?'

'Red.'

'What shape is it?'

'A triangle.'

'Do you know what that means?'

'That the Angels are helping me?'

'Yes.'

At that point, I knew that things were looking rosier and he was now smiling and relaxed. With the ambulance on the way, I stayed with Connor and asked him again, a few minutes later where, what colour and what shape the Angel's healing was. The place and colour was the same but the shape had now become a hexagon.

'Do you know what that means?' I asked him.

'That the Angels are fixing my neck?'

'Yes. Can you ask them when it will be completely fixed?'

'Tomorrow,' Connor said, smiling.

A few minutes later, the ambulance came and my sister announced its arrival to us as it pulled up outside the house.

'Why do I have to go to hospital Uncle Ads?'

'Because they don't know about the Angels and want to see how quickly your neck has got better,' was my improvised reply.

'Can't we just tell them about the Angels?' Connor asked, as if it was the most obvious thing in the World.

My heart melted as I saw the look of genuine bewilderment on his face.

'They don't know about the Angels and want to take you for a ride in the ambulance. Not many boys get to go in the ambulance.'

Connor smiled and his mum took a photo of him strapped to the ambulance trolley. He went to hospital, had his x-ray and was discharged a few hours later – with no residual effects. He was delighted to tell his class at school about his trip to hospital.

Needless to say, I was most relieved that Connor got off unscathed from the incident, and even more pleased that he was delighted with his little adventure.

Young children are a sponge for suggestions and information. It is vital that the information that they get is useful to them. Never was this point illustrated so clearly to me. Connor had accessed his own, innate healing powers, using the Angels as a medium to do so.

I hadn't used my pack of Angel cards before that day but I have certainly used them a few times since – and they have always given me good guidance. It's funny how help comes into my life, from all different ages – and planes of existence.

When have you raised your game under testing circumstances?

There are likely to have already been times in your life where you were forced to find strength or resources that you never knew that you had. Discovering this can be a lifetime quest. You will probably never know the full extent of your capabilities and may, in the light of some of the stories mentioned in this chapter, wish to never be put in a position to find out.

The human body and spirit are capable of some incredible things, which often defy logic. This is when your heart overrules, takes things into its own hands and ignores the limitations and judgements of logic and your head.

You are an incredible individual.

Whether you know this or not, whether you think it or not and whether you believe it or not, there are situations that may or may not happen where you will be able to do incredible things, amaze others and surprise yourself. However, if you spend your whole life playing it safe then you may never discover the hero or heroine inside you that is just waiting for you to embrace it.

> *Exercise: List three times where you have surprised yourself. It doesn't matter how seemingly minor that each instance may appear, as long as it had/has special significance for you. Trust the first things that come to your mind.*

When you have done this, you may be ready to take a leap of faith, which we will look at in the next chapter.

Chapter 16

Take a Leap of Faith

Amongst the many thousands of people who I spoke to who were nearing the end of their lives, the biggest regret I heard was that many of them felt they played their life too safe. They spent plenty of time regretting missed opportunities that appeared uncertain at first sight.

You do not necessarily need to take up skydiving or bungee jumping in order to fulfil this. That said, I can certainly recommend these activities if you are looking for an incredible surge of adrenaline and a feeling of being totally alive and present.

What would you do now if you had no limitations?

Everyone has a calling or urge. Unfortunately, most people also have a well-trained judge, who is an expert at suppressing the verdict, true calling or desire of the heart. Between your unconscious, energetic patterns and programming, your fear and your need to feel safe, this restriction is not always easy to break through. What excites you? What challenges you? What is it that you want to know whether you have the courage to do it or not?

Whom do you love?

There are almost certainly people in your life at the moment, who do not know how much you love them. Whether this is a friend, family member or person that you met and can't stop thinking about, you have probably not told them how you really feel because of one of the following reasons:

- Fear of rejection
- Fear of judgement
- Fear of change

That person may die without ever knowing how you really felt. They may have even been holding back on telling you how much they love you. Yes, there is a chance that the person you love does not love you as much as you do them, but you will never know if you do not take that leap of faith. Unexpressed feelings of love can affect your heart for the rest of your life.

Stories like *Romeo and Juliet* and *West Side Story* are great examples of taking risks in love. The film *Love Actually* is another great example of how good it can be to express how you really feel to someone. If you have seen it, then watch it again and notice how you feel. If you haven't watched it then you are in for a treat.

Would you be prepared to change the fabric of history to follow your heart?

Just imagine what Perry Loving, a white man, and Mildred Jeter, a black woman, must have felt in 1967 when they were married in Washington DC. When they returned to their home state of Virginia, where interracial marriages were illegal, they were swiftly arrested. At court they were told to either spend one year in jail or move to another state. They appealed the decision with the US Supreme Court, forcing a ruling that allowed mixed-race marriages in the USA. They took a leap of faith that could have endangered their lives. What if they had decided that it was too risky?

Perhaps the incident with the biggest ramifications that I know about happened in 1553, when Henry VIII of England decided to defy the entire Catholic Church and divorce his wife. OK, so Henry was a king and had some power but he followed his heart and challenged the most powerful authority in the world at the time. In this case, the centuries of bloodshed that followed as a direct result of this may not be quite such a romantic notion or prove it to be the most cunning plan in the world. Also, the fact that he married six times, executing two of his wives, is hardly the act of a loving heart. In Henry's case, it illustrates that when other people's rules are not working for you, it is your job to change them.

What have you always felt the urge to do?

If the answer to this question involves any sort of damage to anyone else then I urge you to suppress this notion until the higher learning appears. I am only referring to acts that not only benefit you and your heart, but ones that are ecological. By ecological, I mean that they have only a positive impact on you, on anyone involved and on the planet. In the case of Henry VIII, this would certainly not be ecological!

It could be a trip away to a distant land, somewhere that you feel drawn to. It may be a hobby that you have been tempted by in the past, but found an excuse not to go for it. It could be a visit to a friend who you have not seen in a while. Whatever lights up for you now is what your heart wants you to do. What if something happened to you or any of the people involved in your heart's calling? How would you feel if you missed your chance? If you knew that it could never happen, what would that be worth to you then?

Regret is poison for your heart.

So often, I used to hear stories of regret about things that happened decades earlier. Elderly people would sit and recall all of the tiny details of the person or opportunity that they believed would have changed their life in a far more meaningful way. Such memories, which still contain the intensity and emotion as though they just happened yesterday, are like taking a daily dose of poison, which slowly shuts down your heart and will to live.

Regret in itself can be used to ensure that you are open to all other opportunities and possibilities that come your way. However, if it is only used to recall the same incident(s), the same pain and the same sense of missing out then it will slowly kill you emotionally, spiritually, mentally and physically as you progress through your life.

It is the things, people and opportunities that people missed out on, that cause the most pain as health and life start to fade from the physical bodies of people. If you have your health and your heart is calling you to listen then start by feeling it. If it feels good then keep on doing what you are doing. If it doesn't, then change your focus. Know what you want and take a leap of faith.

Not all leaps of faith will give you immediately positive outcomes.

There is always risk involved. This is why it is called a leap of faith. If any doubt enters your head when you have made the leap then it can affect the result that you get. There will be uncertainty, there will be challenges and there will be other opportunities that present themselves. How quickly you can adjust to circumstances that change quickly will affect the results that you get. That said, you might be lucky and find that everything goes smoothly to plan. If this happens then you have cause for celebration.

Before they were famous.

If you are thinking that there is no way that you could take a leap of faith just yet, just consider where some of today's big celebrities have come from and what they must have had to do to get where they are. Brad Pitt once dressed up in a chicken suit for a fast food restaurant. Rod Stewart was once a gravedigger. Christopher Walken was once a circus lion tamer. Sean Connery worked as a milkman. Whoopi Goldberg used to put makeup on corpses at a mortuary. Hugh Jackman was once a clown. Ozzy Osbourne worked in a slaughterhouse and Madonna once worked at Dunkin' Donuts.

Whatever you are doing now, you may only be one leap of faith away from an extraordinary life.

If you never take the leap, then you'll never know.

J. K. Rowling was a single mother, earning barely enough money to pay for food and rent. She didn't even have the money for a second-hand typewriter. After 12 rejections from publishing houses, Bloomsbury Press eventually accepted her. Even then, her publisher advised her to get another job, as 'You'll never make any money out of children's books.'

What would have happened to her if she hadn't taken the leap of faith?

Exercise: If you had to take a leap of faith, what would it be and why? Feel free to write this down. Once you've done that write down three small steps you could take towards it, regardless of how seemingly far away from the goal that they are.

In the next chapter, we will lighten things up a bit.

Chapter 17

Common Sense Does Not Exist

Have you ever used the term, 'Common sense'?

If you have then it was probably a comment following something stupid that someone did, to express what appears blatantly obvious or to counteract a stupid question that you were asked. Despite advancements in technology, science and understanding, the capacity for human beings to bypass the seemingly obvious, sensible option is limitless.

A friend, and charge nurse in the Psychiatric Intensive Care Unit at the time, once listened to me complain. I was talking about the degree of stupidity, dogma and ridiculousness that a shift as a nurse in the National Health Service (NHS) could bring. After listening to my musings he smiled and told me that, 'Common sense in the NHS does not exist.' Not only did this start to make sense of my time working in a hospital, it also made sense for much of my life.

I once wrote an article titled *Common sense does not exist*. I briefly highlighted some of the points that I will make in this chapter. One person wrote a comment saying, 'Common sense does exist; it just doesn't happen very often.' This statement proved my point wonderfully. Common sense is an oxymoron, or contradiction in terms. Sense exists but it is rarely common. What is common to one person is different in most others.

In my brief time working as a waiter, there were certain dishes that came straight out of the oven and were scalding hot. Although I would put these dishes on a cooler plate and say, 'Be careful, the plate is hot,' to my customers, at least half of them would feel the need to touch the plate to check, often giving themselves a nasty burn. These same people, who probably had responsible jobs, making informed decisions at work all day, would be guilty of the same errors. I have been one of those people.

When did you last witness something stupid?

What was it that caused you to wonder what must go on in someone's head to do what they do? Maybe it was a YouTube video, a hidden camera or something that you have seen in your everyday life. There are always people doing stupid things. Common sense to an electrician is not to touch a live wire, yet a non-electrician may not realise this. To a plumber it is common sense not to flush too many wipes or solid objects down a toilet, yet pipes are blocked everyday by those who have not yet learned this lesson. As a nurse, I was constantly amazed, indeed, I still am, at how so few people hydrate themselves properly, despite our body being about 70% water. All of these things could be considered sense, yet they are not common.

If you wish to understand the full potential for human stupidity then look up 'The Darwin Awards' on the internet. Here you will find endless stories of where sense is not only not common, it is completely absent. To highlight the point, during the world Coronavirus crisis people tagged toilet roll as the primary target for what to stock up on. Mass stupidity is real so it's insane to expect people to act rationally all of the time. If they do it some of the time then that's a step in the right direction!

In April 1995, Timothy O'Brien committed suicide by shooting himself in the head because he thought his lottery numbers had come in on a week that he had forgotten to buy a ticket. As if this story isn't tragic enough, even if the ticket was valid, he wouldn't have won. He would only have won £47 as only four of his usual numbers had come in. Mr O'Brien had made a mistake.

On 29 September 1929, John and Myrtle Bennet were hosting their friends Charles and Myrna Hoffman for a friendly game of bridge, in Kansas City. A dispute about who should have played what card led to an argument and to Myrtle Bennet shooting her husband as he attempted to flee the apartment, killing him dead. What is perhaps even more nonsensical about this case is that, despite taking four shots at her husband and hitting him with two of them, Mrs Bennet was acquitted on the grounds that the shooting of her husband was accidental.

In January 2009 in Pennsylvania, a 17-year-old boy found an M-80 explosive firecracker at his grandmother's house and took it to his room to examine it. He began repeatedly lighting and extinguishing the fuse until one time it would not go out. His not-so-cunning solution was to place the device between his thighs and cover it with his hand, in order to muffle the explosion. A few seconds later, our young experimenter had lost his right hand, right leg and right to reproduce. On reflection, this may have been to the benefit of the gene pool.

It doesn't just affect the young.

Back in July 2008 in Italy, Gerhard, a 68-year-old man, drove his car onto a rail track, causing the car to get stuck. With a train heading towards him, his solution involved getting out of the car and running along the track towards the oncoming train. He did not want it to hit his car. Although the train slowed down as a result of this action, causing less damage to the car, Gerhard forgot to move out of the way and was hurtled 30 metres through the air. Attempts to revive him were unsuccessful.

Incredible acts of mindlessness happen every day.

In January 2005 in Croatia, 55-year-old Marko had an idea for a chimney-cleaning tool. His device involved a brush, a chain and a metal object to weigh down the brush. He would stand on the roof and lower the brush down the chimney. As he set about welding the metal object to the brush, he appeared to have overlooked that the metal object was, in fact, a grenade. The explosion killed Marko instantly, blasting shrapnel through the walls of the shed and the windscreen of a Mercedes that was parked outside.

If your jaw is dropping at the overwhelming idiocy of some of these stories then take a look at 'The Darwin Awards' and read some more for yourself. This section could fill an encyclopaedia.

You may well be wondering how it is possible that so many people waive their right to act in a way that common sense would seem to dictate, if it really existed. This is an interesting question and, from my origins at the lunatic asylum, I am not sure that my opinion is the most valid. However, I will do my best to throw some light on this intriguing aspect of human behaviour.

We act with emotion and justify with logic.

Looking to make sense of life and human behaviour is futile, at best. You are an emotional being and there are certain sets of circumstances that will make you do things that you could never believe possible. Part of this is due to other people's energetic patterns that are running in you, which we discussed in chapter 14. The rest is caused by a jailbreak, which we have discussed in chapter 5. Both of these factors will override logic, causing behaviour that can be anything from slightly odd to completely insane.

Because your judge, or head, likes to think it's in control, it is then common to create some sort of explanation as to why you acted the way that you did. When you have a jailbreak there is no logic, it is just the result of a courtroom that has been run by an unfair judge for far too long.

Do what I say, not what I do.

How often have you heard this utterly insane suggestion? We are creatures who learn by copying what we see others do, especially as children. Being told not to do something that is unfolding in front of you is just not a logical request. This is the logic that sees health professionals tell patients to give up smoking, moments before they go outside the ward for a cigarette. It is the same logic that parents use to tell their children never to drink alcohol, as they sit down giggling with a glass of wine in their hand. The same logic that warns others to always have safe sex, before taking a risk because there are no condoms available and the moment seemed too good to miss out on.

Let the person who has never sinned cast the first stone.

I am not, or never have been, a religious man. My dad grew up in Belfast and made sure that I had nothing to do with anything religious whilst I was growing up. My grandad's best friend converted religion to marry. One was Catholic, the other Protestant. They were so close that my dad grew up calling my grandad's friend Niall his uncle. Being told that they should not like each other on religious grounds was never going to carry any weight in my family.

There are, however, a few phrases I have heard from the bible that resonate, and casting stones is one of them. Having been that hypocrite on more than one occasion, I offer no judgement towards you, or anyone else. This is simply my observation of life's lunatic asylum.

If you are honest, you can recall at least one occasion where you acted as a hypocrite. It may have been that you were giving advice that you were not taking at the time. You may have complained about behaviour that you have displayed earlier. You may even have deliberately set out to hurt someone, before being outraged when someone did it back to you. It is this factor that can lead ex-drinkers and ex-smokers taking exception to anyone who they see repeating their old actions.

Negotiating life logically is just not sensible.

For all of the courtrooms in the world, there is unlikely to ever be a judge that runs a fair and congruent court on a consistent basis. Every news story that upsets you, every person who presses your buttons and every incident that causes you to explode onto your soap box, is life's lunatic asylum looking to keep you a prisoner within its walls.

Learn to let go and flow.

Holding on to judgement and blame is a bit like flowing down a wild, rock-laden, river backwards. As you sit looking at the rocks that you have just hit, waving your paddle at them in outrage, getting worked up and blaming them for hitting you, you are missing the chance to steer out of the way of those approaching. Some people spend their whole life so focused on what has just happened that they fail to see what is happening to them in the here and now.

Logically, your head is always looking for answers, whilst your heart just wants to flow to a place that feels good, from moment-to-moment. This is not easy if you are focusing on what has just happened, rather than where you are right now and what is approaching.

Barking mad.

I used to work night shifts in acute medical settings. When there is a full moon, it plays havoc with some people, especially elderly folk with infections and/or breathing difficulties. Had I not seen things go crazy consistently on a full moon during over ten years of night shifts, I would never have believed it.

I would sit down with dear, sweet patients who would be smiling and polite at 22.00 in the evening. By 01.00 in the morning, they could be doing anything from screaming abuse at me or the other patients, walking naked through the ward, urinating on other patients, to singing and waking up everyone else. I have witnessed all of these things.

On one occasion, a Lord was admitted to my ward. He ended up barricading himself in the ward office and throwing furniture at the windows to escape. When I left the ward that morning there were three porters, four policemen and the hospital site manager looking to get through his office barricade. Watching some people turn from models of politeness to rebels, voicing language that was fit only for the gutter, amused me no end.

Each morning the patients in question would return to their former selves, with no recollection of anything that had happened during the night. On the few occasions that I attempted to point out what had gone on, they would not believe me.

I would not have believed it if I hadn't seen it so many times.

Whatever you think will or will not happen to you when or if you get much older, you probably have no idea. The fact is that illness can be a very strange thing for some. I often wondered how it was possible that the moon could have such an effect on human behaviour. The origin of the word luna(r)tic started to make sense to me. When you think that we are 70% water and the effect that the moon has on the ocean then there is some possible reason.

My lunacy in the NHS.

I could make a separate book out of this subject, just with my experiences alone. However, I will resist my temptation to completely expose the full degree of ludicrousness that I saw during my time as a nurse.

One night I was working on an acute medical ward, where a particularly nasty bug had spread, called Pseudo-Membranous Colitis (PMC). Because it had proliferated so quickly and was so nasty, the hospital microbiologist closed our ward to admissions. At this stage 8 of the 23 patients on the ward had the bug.

That night it turned out that the only available bed in the hospital was in our ward, in a four-bedded bay, where the other three patients all had PMC. Amongst them was a confused lady who would wander around the other beds, touching the patients, making infection-control almost impossible. Indeed, she was almost certainly responsible for the rapid spread of the infection on the ward.

Pressure from above.

The government had taken firm measures to increase hospital efficiency. Their initiative for reducing waiting times in hospital Accident and Emergency (A&E) departments was to fine any hospital £50,000 and conduct an enquiry for every patient who was kept in A&E for longer than 12 hours. To prevent this from happening an executive decision was made from the Senior Nurse

Manager in the Trust to open the bed in our infected bay so as not to incur the government-inspired repercussions. We were to admit a lady in her 90s with severe pneumonia.

Despite vociferous objections by the staff on the ward, we were overruled and forced to accept the patient. I wrote an email to the decision-maker, complaining about the situation. A few days later, the new admission was dead and died shortly after an episode of PMC-infected diarrhoea, which she had been passing regularly since contracting it shortly after her arrival. Because this lady had no relatives, her death could be swept under the carpet.

I did not receive a reply to my email until after the lady was dead. The decision-maker in question claimed to have not been told of the full circumstances. This was despite clear facts presented by the ward staff to the hospital manager at the time. The hospital was certainly running more efficiently, just not in a way that everyone appreciated. This was the reality of what we had to cope with on the wards.

Such lunacy in the NHS, as a result of government targets and 'breakdowns in communication', were a daily reality of my life as a nurse.

To attribute blame to individuals in the wake of such incidents proved to be as stressful as it was utterly pointless at times. Being surrounded by such lunacy made me realise that the psychiatric hospital I had grown up in was the best training that I could have had to prepare me for my career as a nurse.

Death from within.

Illness and death are a part of life. Witnessing the living dead is not a pleasant experience. I could cite many cases but will use my great uncle as an example. He grew up fighting during the Second World War. Like many of his generation, he lived a very frugal life. He saved money from his pension, of about £70 per week. When he went in for a routine operation on his knee, he experienced 'complications' during the procedure. In this case he developed Compartment Syndrome due to the surgery. This is a painful condition caused by increased pressure in the muscles building to dangerous levels and restricting blood flow. These 'complications' led to him requiring continuous care for the rest of his life and never being able to walk for more than a minute at a time again.

When he was 'fit' to leave the hospital, he was sent to a nursing home for the rest of his life. Because he had saved money all of his life, he was required to pay over £500 per week to receive care following his operational misadventure. This knowledge and his perceived poor treatment by the staff of the home, all on minimum wages, contributed significantly to his diminished sense of morale, killing him slowly from within. He died within a few months of 'natural causes.'

I witnessed hundreds of similar cases to that of my great uncle. When some people take a permanent dip in their independence through an inability to look after their basic health needs, they stop living. Their body may still be alive but mentally, they are already dead.

Do you own your own assets?

If you do then the same fate may well await you if you live in the UK. I cannot comment on how this gambit would evolve overseas, though I suspect that there are many similar cases. The realisation that your life has come down to spending your final days dependent on others, devoid of the ability to look after yourself, can cause extreme mental taxation. Knowing that your savings are being drained away as you pay premium rates for minimum wage care is a death in itself to the elderly people who grew up during a war, saving all of their lives so that they had money to pass on to their loved ones. This can lead to a heavy heart and a cornucopia of regret.

Consequently, I spent my NHS years feeling reticent about the benefits of owning my own house and being subjected to a life of nursing to pay for it. Not that I was ever able to seriously consider owning my own house in London on a nursing wage. It is my intention for you to at least think about what you expect from the future, and how you will reflect upon your life if you live long enough to witness your ability to look after yourself slip away.

I do not tell you any of this to condemn or criticise the NHS or any other country's system of health. Looking after the health of individuals is, ultimately, the responsibility of each of us throughout our lives. To blame anyone is futile at best. The NHS provides free healthcare for the country's residents. This is a good thing. I have discussed earlier how such judgement can only lead to the manifestation of heart disease.

I tell you this in an attempt to shock you into thinking about where you are now with your health and consider what it is worth to you.

So many people spend their lives sacrificing their health for money. At what point will you decide that your health and wellbeing are worth investing in?

What would you pay to avoid the possible scenario of my great uncle for an extra year or two of vibrant health? If you are already taking your health and wellbeing seriously then I commend you for your good sense. If not, this is common, and the exercise at the end of this chapter could be a life-altering one for you.

On a lighter note.

Since we all die anyway and you will not know how, right up until it happens, you may as well just enjoy your health while you can. Watching Monty Python's *Life of Brian* is the perspective that I choose to take right now. By cultivating luck, realising that we live in a lunatic asylum and making a few small lifestyle adjustments, it is possible to enjoy your life more in the here and now.

This is not to say that I lead a perfectly healthy life. I am not perfect by any stretch of the imagination. What I think of myself as is perfectly imperfect. This involves loving the part of myself that likes to do things that many health purists could deem unwise. The day that you love yourself, whatever you do, you will improve your state of wellbeing immeasurably.

Exercise: Imagine that it is your funeral. How many people's lives did you affect? How many do you think will turn up? Who is a significant figure or focus of your attention in your life at the moment who will almost certainly not bother attending? What do you think will be said about you and how many people will bother to speak? How do you think you will be remembered? What influence or legacy will you leave?

It will help to write down this exercise and give it lengthy consideration. You may wish to add what you will commit to doing in order to align this occasion with your expectations.

I realise that things have been a bit heavy in this chapter, so allow me to lighten things up in the next.

Chapter 18

Humour is Essential

When a psychotic patient was about to die on an acute psychiatric ward in the west of Ireland, a priest was called in to give him his last rites. This is standard practice in Ireland.

The priest walked up to the dying man's bed and asked him, 'Do you renounce the devil and all of his sin?' There was a long, uncertain silence as the dying man opened his eyes wide, with a tortured look, whilst the nurses in the room looked on.

The priest repeated his question. This time with a little more volume, 'Do you renounce the devil and all of his sin?'

Once again, there was a long pause. The dying man's nostrils flared and his eyes opened wide once again. The nurses looked at each other in wonder at how this gambit would play out.

For a third time, the priest asked vociferously, 'Do you renounce the devil and all of his sin?'

The dying man grabbed the priest's arm and tensed his grip, like a vice. His eyes puffed out as he said, 'This is not a time for me to be making enemies.'

The nurses laughed and the priest was stunned. The man died shortly afterwards.

This is a true story. When it was told to me by one of the nurses in the room, and very good friend, we were laughing for a long time. We also debated the benefits of letting priests loose with dying, psychotic patients. Being able to take comedy from even the darkest situations is a lesson that does not always sink in instantly.

When life gets heavy and you feel as though you would just like the ground to open up and swallow you, knowing that you will eventually be able to laugh about it is a true gift. And having friends that can do this for you is invaluable. This does not always happen quickly or with every situation that ever challenges you, though it can get easier the more that you do it.

We are all shaped by our past. During three years of training as a student nurse, there had always been someone around who was more senior and experienced than I on the ward. If something potentially serious happened, I could always let someone else lead the call. I felt safe.

After three weeks of being qualified, I was working on a busy medical ward. When the two most senior nurses decided to go for a morning coffee break together and leave the ward, I was faced with my first ever instance of being the most senior nurse. Leaving a newly qualified nurse in charge would generally be considered less than ideal practice but it was not my decision.

Phones were ringing, patients were demanding my attention, people needed washing, drugs needed to be administered, relatives were demanding updates on patients that I had not even met, and porters were arriving to take patients away for tests, without even letting me know.

This was my life as a newly qualified nurse.

I felt under-qualified, unready and very apprehensive at this prospect. I had never been present for a life or death situation that didn't have someone around who had led a similar situation before. Yes, I had been given all of the theory and attended resuscitation workshops but I'd never had to do the real thing. I had looked on as a student but that was miles from what was about to happen to me.

When a cleaner strolled over to me and casually mentioned that there was a patient on the toilet who didn't look too well, I went straight to the cubicle. The cleaner was clearly a master of the understatement.

There was a patient dead on the toilet.

Unless you have been in this situation, it is difficult to describe what happened next. It started with a whirlwind of terror, shock, panic and adrenaline. In this, my first ever cardiac arrest situation that I was in charge of, the man was clearly very dead and any attempt to change that would be futile. However, the fusion of panic and hospital procedure can be a funny thing.

I asked one Care Assistant to call the resuscitation team and lifted the dead man from the toilet to his bed, on the other side of the ward, with the other Care Assistant. All of the other patients on the ward and their visiting relatives could see us carry him, as it was an open-plan ward. It must have been a surreal sight for them, watching two nurses run across the ward with a dead man but I didn't have time to think about anything else at that point. It was more *Benny Hill* than *ER*! All I knew was that the handover I received did not give me any reason to believe that the man wasn't alive and relatively well.

The man was cold, white, stiff and very dead.

He had died on the toilet with a huge, anal bleed. What made it worse was that he must have been there, undetected, since the shift before. I know this as he had rigor mortis, which takes at least four hours, usually longer, to set in. I had been on the ward for about an hour and a half. I did not get a full handover because I started an hour later than the rest of the staff that shift. This was part of an initiative to save the hospital money. They saved less than £10 that day on my wages. This was clearly worth the saving for me not getting a proper handover on that particular occasion.

As the resuscitation team arrived, imagine their surprise and my horror to find that we could not lay this man flat because he had rigor mortis.

He had stiffened so that his legs were at a ninety-degree angle. The fact that I had placed an airway in his mouth, an oxygen mask on him and had started the resuscitation process must have looked utterly ridiculous to the team as they rushed through the curtains and looked on in bewilderment. The dead man's knees narrowly missed my head as he rocked during my cardiac compressions on his chest. I swiftly realised that this must have looked ludicrous, as the aghast resuscitation team stared at me.

I was filled with panic. Hospital procedure stated that if someone is for resuscitation then an emergency call MUST go out when a patient's heart ceases to beat. It is not usually expected that there will be at least a four-hour delay for this to happen.

I felt utterly humiliated.

I was subjected to some cutting questions from the doctor in the resuscitation team. My friends laughed at me, as did the senior nurses. I was devastated and terrified to go back to work after this incident. At first, I perceived their humour as insensitive. However, I eventually saw the funny side, knowing that the night staff should have realised that he was dead before they left the ward, and the rest of the staff on the shift with me had failed to identify that he was dead during the hour before I arrived. Nothing that I could have done would change these facts.

I learned several key lessons very fast.

1. Locate ALL of your patients at the beginning of each shift.
2. Treat all handovers with at least a hint of caution.
3. Shit happens, and for some it's much worse than for others.
4. Dealing with death is easier when you learn to see the funny side of things.
5. When you start at the deep end, it gets easier from that point onwards.

Afterwards some of my colleagues would call me over to clearly dead patients and ask if I wanted to attempt resuscitation before they sent them to the mortuary. There were many laughs at my expense as a result of that incident. Allied with my experience of a psychiatric patient exploding diarrhoea on my foot a day earlier, as I lifted him out of the bath, and the time that my colleague forgot to unhook a patient's catheter before we rolled them over, flicking infected urine all over my face and chest as the catheter disconnected from its bag, I provided many laughs for my colleagues.

By accepting that my colleagues would laugh at me ruthlessly, I was able to laugh at them and the numerous ridiculous episodes that I witnessed as a nurse. This made the job better and cheered me up in many situations that may have caused others to break down.

I went on to witness hundreds of people die, see some tragic things and reflect on many life-changing incidents. In each case, it was important to remain calm and cope with whatever situation arose. From babies dying with meningitis to patching together dead bodies from traffic accidents before escorting the relatives in to see them, nursing in an acute setting and breaking bad news to people can be a life-shaping experience.

Everyone has a different coping mechanism.

What is your coping mechanism? Do you tell your friends or keep it to yourself? What strategy do you adopt so that you can proceed with your life, when inside you can feel the walls crumbling? In many situations, mine is humour. People adopt a host of different strategies to cope with stress.

Some shout and stress others, some say nothing, some cry, pretend it never happened, get depressed or even get suicidal. Some of my colleagues did not cope particularly well as nurses when stress levels rose, killing themselves, some deliberately and some by accident. If you have ever felt depressed or suicidal then you know what I am talking about. Sometimes life will ride you roughshod and leave you battered and bruised.

Death has always been at hand to remind me of the impermanence of my life and friendships.

You or your loved ones could be dead any day. You will not always get a warning before it happens. The consequence of all of my nursing experiences has been to teach me that I can enjoy life whilst I have it. What could you do to enjoy your life more right now?

I appreciate my friends and family always. I learn to laugh at as much as I can, as quickly as possible, and I will do my best to forgive those who feel the need to pass judgement on me. This isn't always easy and sometimes takes longer than usual for me. Being told when I should laugh and when I shouldn't by others has become a part of my life. It may be a part of yours. Sometimes people will pass judgement upon you, without knowing the full facts, the coping mechanism in action or bigger picture at work. Laughing at something does not mean that you don't care any more than getting upset doesn't mean that you have no sense of humour.

Ultimately, life is too short to spend feeling bad or blaming and judging others for things that cannot be changed. Everything in life offers us an opportunity to learn, improve and move forward with more knowledge and experience. Learning to laugh and move on is the way of your heart.

Nursing was never going to be a financially rewarding career for me, and neither would it cater for any sensitive souls who like to feel good all of the time. What nursing did for me was acquaint me with the ephemeral nature of life, moods, logic and drugs. Stress causes different people to adopt different coping mechanisms. There is always a choice of what you can think and feel while you are alive. One day, death will visit us all. Will you fear death or love your life?

What could you be seeing the brighter side of at the moment?

With the friend network that I have, I can be assured that whenever a major tragedy occurs there will be a humorous text message just a few minutes away.

You may even think this may not exactly be the archetypal, caring act. This is understandable. We all function differently, even amongst nurses.

Whether you think humour is appropriate or not, it will always have a place. It has also been proved that those who are faster to look on the more humorous side of life will cope with life better.

I was once working as a student on a medical ward when a 43-year-old man was admitted for tests after experiencing some abdominal pain. In typically male fashion it had been a problem for about a week but he had a construction contract that he wanted to finish before 'getting it sorted'. I would sit down and chat with him and found out that he was a life-long football fan and supporter of Leyton Orient. I had assessed whether he was open to a joke or two and felt that he was. Consequently we had a day of banter before I came into work the next day.

During handover that day I was told that the test results were back and that he had been diagnosed with pancreatic cancer, which had spread to his bowel. The spread was so bad that it had been considered inoperable. He had effectively been handed a death sentence as far as the doctors were concerned.

I had no idea what to say to him when I first went over to speak to him that shift. I simply sat next to him and said that I had heard the news and was so sorry to hear it. He thanked me and sat in silence for a minute. I simply sat with him. Eventually he looked at me and asked what his chances of surviving much longer were.

When I told him that his chances were better than Leyton Orient's of winning the league, we both started laughing.

The senior nurse on the ward swiftly walked across the ward, demanding that I followed her into the office. She then reprimanded me for *laughing inappropriately* with a terminally ill patient. When I asked what constituted inappropriate laughter, I was not given an explanation by my stern mentor that was anywhere close to convincing. Consequently, I went on to write an assignment about laughter on the wards, researching what was known. I did offer to let the nurse in question read my completed assignment but she chose not to.

There is a phenomenal weight of evidence on the healing power of laughter.

I wrote a full assignment on this subject alone. However, I will mention one person who I found during my research: a chap called Norman Cousins.

He had used humour and large doses of vitamin C to combat heart disease, before developing crippling arthritis, which gave him continuous pain. His pain was so bad that he had been unable to even sleep properly.

He discovered that by watching *The Marx Brothers* and inducing a belly laugh for ten minutes, he would get a few hours of pain-free sleep. Laughter was a better painkiller than any prescription drug that he was given. He went on to write about his experiences and become a strong advocate of humour in a medical setting.

I found plenty to back up what Norman Cousins had to say and continued to laugh on the ward when I deemed it appropriate. There were certainly occasions when my instinct told me that laughter was not the best approach for certain patients, in some situations. I found that I developed a pretty good gauge for who was receptive to having a laugh. I would joke with patients regularly, speaking loud enough that it would spread to others, getting them in on the joke. Do you get a sense of who is open to more humour in your life?

What makes you laugh?

Maybe it's a joke, series, comedian, person or film. Whatever it is, access it more often. I am constantly drawn back to Monty Python's *Holy Grail* and *Life of Brian*. The song, *Always Look on the Bright Side of Life*, is one of my favourites. Often, when faced with grim situations I would start to sing this and change the energy and mood of those around me. What if you learned to do the same, quickly turning a heavy, dense, draining, problem-driven situation into a joke? I have found this to be a great way of managing my own energy and that of others during such situations.

Whether it sounds like a feasible option for you at the moment or not, this is a powerful technique when used effectively. However, there are other ways of making light of certain situations, which not only cheer you up, but also help you cheer up others.

Dealing with rejection.

Whilst I have plenty of experience in this field, I found a great example of someone doing something totally different, which made me laugh. Here is a response to a rejection letter that I found:

Herbert A. Millington
Chair - Search Committee
412A Clarkson Hall, Whitson University
College Hill, MA 34109

Dear Professor Millington,

Thank you for your letter of 16 March. After careful consideration, I regret to inform you that I am unable to accept your refusal to offer me an assistant professor position in your department.

This year I have been particularly fortunate in receiving an unusually large number of rejection letters. With such a varied and promising field of candidates, it is impossible for me to accept all refusals.

Despite Whitson's outstanding qualifications and previous experience in rejecting applicants, I find that your rejection does not meet my needs at this time. Therefore, I will assume the position of assistant professor in your department this August. I look forward to seeing you then.

Best of luck in rejecting future applicants.

Sincerely,
Chris L. Jensen

What a great way to take rejection and alchemise it in a way that makes yourself and others laugh. Chris L. Jensen may not have been accepted for the job but he has certainly made plenty of friends and made a few people smile with his approach to rejection.

Free and natural drugs!

Smiling and laughter release serotonin, your body's natural, feel–good drug. It helps you to feel better, you don't need a dealer or prescription, it's legal and gives you an instant fix. The good news is that even if you are thinking that there is nothing to smile or laugh about at the moment, you can still benefit. By holding even a false smile, your brain does not know the difference and will release serotonin anyway.

Not feeling good and holding a false smile may take some getting used to and maybe feel a bit strange but it is easy to do and far gentler on your body than most of the alternatives. Give it a go. You may even like it.

> *Exercise: Hold a smile for at least a minute, preferably longer. If you wish to watch or listen to something that helps, then do so. Notice how you feel inside your body, even if you are not feeling great to begin with. If you want to take it a step further, hold your arms in the air, stretched up above your head, for at least 1 minute, longer if you find yourself enjoying it. Notice how you feel after.*

When you have done this, we will look at the rules of your life, examine who created them and assess whether any of them need to be changed.

Chapter 19

The Rules of Your Life

You are here to play.

Life is a game and you are here to play it. How you play it, is up to you. Will you learn the rules, changing any that you don't like and enjoy it; or play without knowing the rules, and hope that you can make sense of it as you go? If you do this, then whose rules will you believe?

So many people are playing life's game to other people's rules. You can make your own. When you do, you will find that there are other people who want to play with you because they think your rules are good. Anyone who doesn't like your rules can always go and play with someone else.

Do things that stretch your comfort zone and feel good.

The best games involve chance. What would you love to do but have not yet had the nerve? It is easy not to do the things you love. Becoming comfortable in discomfort is a common, if dangerous, game to play. If you're not enjoying your life then your heart is suffering. Whilst there are no quick fixes on your journey to discovering some sort of purpose in your life, there are a few things that are great fun, if a little nerve racking at first.

I was once asked to set up a free hug stand for Mental Health Awareness week. The idea of hugging complete strangers seemed odd at first. Standing on the streets of London offering free hugs has elicited comments from, 'If you do I'll break your nose' and 'I'm not gay,' to 'What a wonderful thing to do' and 'Is it alright if I join you?' The fun and connection generated by a group of people giving out free hugs is something that is very good for your heart. Even though it clearly brought up a few issues for a very small minority, some of the people who were not quite so friendly have given me a smile or two.

When I first did this, an old lady with a Zimmer frame approached me. She had to squint through the thick lenses of her glasses to read the sign that I was holding, slowly moving closer to me.

'Does that say free hugs dear?' she asked me.

'Yes it does. Would you like a free hug?' I replied.

'I'd love a free hug,' she said. I hugged her for about a minute. She was not letting go so I kept going. She then started to cry.

'Are you alright?' I asked her.

'I'm sorry dear. My husband died three years ago and nobody has hugged me since.'

I had just given out free hugs for a bit of fun at first. At this moment, I realised that I had done something meaningful, which had made a big difference in someone's life. Had it not been for this incident I may never have done free hugs again. The act of spreading good will, having fun and changing the rules of life has been great. What do you do that feels good?

I went to London on Christmas Eve for a few years, giving out free hugs. The goal was to get hugs from people from all around the world. One year a small group of us managed to cover six continents (we haven't hugged anyone from Antarctica yet) and have a great time. We have been given free food and free drinks by people who loved what we were doing, and made many people smile. What could you do to have more fun and maybe make yourself and a few people smile?

Whose rules are you playing your life by?

If you find yourself not loving your life right now then start to look at the rules that you are using. It is common to adopt family rules. Doing things because your family want you to play by their rules was a frequent underlying issue with people whom I have spoken to. Doing jobs because of what was expected from one's family is great, unless you don't love it. People sometimes get stuck in careers that can turn their heart into a lunatic, when your body's courtroom continuously ignores its call. This is a jailbreak just waiting to happen, building like a pressure cooker.

Societal rules.

Societal rules, for the many in the Western world, are generally something along the line of, 'Get a good job, buy a house, save a pension, find a life-partner, have kids and fit in if you want to get along in life.' So many people do this, only to find that there is something missing in their lives. It is this game that can contribute to the symptoms of a mid-life crisis (which appears to be happening at younger ages now). This happens after years of playing a game that you do not like.

Would you play a computer game or board game that you didn't like because you thought it would get better in a few decades time? You probably think that this is a stupid question to ask, yet, this is what so many people do with their lives, before ending up in hospital with critical conditions.

Buying things on credit that tie people to jobs and work is another aspect of life that can affect your heart health. The amount of people who buy things that they don't really need, with money that they don't really have, to please or keep up with people that they don't even like, is staggering. Because of the increasingly reckless attitude of money-lending agencies, many people are borrowing beyond their means and then living a life of debt-related stress. The objects that are being bought (often to make the buyers feel better) have the reverse effect if they cannot be paid for easily. Cars, holidays, extensions on houses and new furniture are a few prime examples.

National rules.

In the case of the UK, where I grew up, national rules are open to interpretation. I only offer my angle on how I perceive some of our rules:

- Don't kill anyone because that's a terrible sin and you will go to jail for it. (Unless you join our armed forces, and if we interfere with another country's affairs and decide to go to war with them. In that case, kill your fellow men without getting to know them, even though they could be your friends otherwise. We will supply you with the weapons.)
- Pay your taxes and serve your country and your country will serve you. (Unless you are old, very ill and have no relatives, in which case you may not be served quite so well.)
- Only tell the truth, the whole truth and nothing but the truth. (Unless you are a senior government official, in which case it is acceptable to lie as we may not be able to handle the truth.)
- Save plenty of money for your retirement. (So that we can use it to pay for your care if you get ill, thus saving your country money to spend on more weapons.)

- Recycle and be greener in your choices. (While we develop more powerful and lethal weapons and test them randomly, in order to keep us all safe.)
- And everybody has their own spin on the Coronavirus pandemic. (Be alert, stay responsible, but make sure you have as much toilet roll as you can carry.)

I realise that I have been pretty flippant and maybe just slightly controversial with this section. I also realise that this by no means paints a full picture. I just want you to start thinking about whose rules that you are using. Whose life are you really living and how much of your life are you currently happy with?

What rules will you use?

You can change every situation in your life, when you are ready for it to happen. If you are not happy in your job, start looking for another and be open to new possibilities. If it means having less money, then start considering how you could adjust. If you are not happy in your relationship, get professional help to see if you have any chance of making it work, or leave. If you cannot see any way out of your current situation, start asking for help and connecting with people who have been through what you are going through. If life appears meaningless, then find a purpose to drive you forward. Get help. So many people do not even ask.

So many people overestimate what they can achieve in a week and underestimate what they can achieve in a year. If you have ever been on a diet that didn't work or made a New Year's resolution that had been broken by February, then you know what I'm talking about. If you are not happy with yourself then do something to move in the right direction and commit to at least ten minutes every day of something that will move you towards a better place. Over a year, that will add up to over 60 hours of activity to make your life better. Imagine the possibilities of what can happen to you in 60 hours of focused positive action.

It is your life and your rulebook.

Are you going to make things happen, watch what happens, or wonder what happened? Regardless of how bad you have had it and what you think has held you back, the only person who can make your life better is you. To do that you may well need to change your rules and take action.

In 1950, Mother Teresa founded the Missionaries of Charity, in Calcutta, India. She then spent 45 years of her life looking after the poor, sick, orphaned and dying, whilst guiding other missionaries to do the same. Following an insight that she had in 1946 to leave the convent and live amongst the poor and sick, she would make her mark on the world.

A more recent example is Greta Thunberg. One school student was able to mobilise hundreds of thousands of people globally because she felt so strongly about climate change. Just one impassioned speech was enough to put her on the world map and get her in front of leaders all over the globe. Love her or hate her, she proved that one person can make a difference when they are prepared to step up and be counted.

The call of humanity, from within the lunacy.

The First World War started over the killing of Archduke Franz Ferdinand of Austria. Amongst a series of spectacular cock-ups, his car took a wrong turn and accidentally reversed past a despondent assassin, who thought he had missed his chance. The assassin could not believe his luck as the car backed up in front of where he was sitting. He swiftly shot the Archduke and was then killed by the accompanying troops. Maybe the assassin was not so lucky.

This one, isolated incident led to a World War. Suddenly, millions of men were told to kill each other by various world leaders, who had been making secret treaties. Over 16 million died and over 21 million were wounded as a result of one man's actions. If this was not an act of madness, then what was? Without question, people of the world were prepared to die because of the disagreements between a handful of people who decided that war was the only answer (who you can be sure were never going to volunteer to join their men on any of the suicidal charges into No Man's Land.)

Humanity from insanity.

Just imagine being in the trenches in December 1914 and being one of the first troops to enter No Man's Land, to speak to people who you had been trying to kill. The same people who had also wanted to kill you. This single act of breaking the rules has become iconic over the years. The game of football that was played following this is perhaps the most significant game in history.

Despite having no official truce, German troops began decorating the area around their trenches near Ypres in Belgium, lighting candles and singing Christmas carols. The British returned Christmas carols until troops from each side entered No Man's Land to swap stories and gifts. The troops had to be moved to different positions afterwards because they refused to shoot at each other.

Regardless of how challenging life can appear, you always have the option of changing the rules.

If you don't like the game of life that you are playing at the moment then start by asking what needs to change. Just because certain options would take you well out of your comfort zone, just think what the price will be if everything stayed the same in your life for the rest of your days. This is the sort of lifestyle that turns many into the living dead in their latter years. They rue the chances that they could have taken, beating themselves up for playing it so safe.

Easy, predictable games are often boring.

Tic-tac-toe, or crosses and noughts as it is otherwise known, is the equivalent of a predictable game to anyone who has played it regularly. After a relatively small learning curve it becomes impossible to win because of the relatively small number of options available. How long would you be prepared to play such a game? Indeed, what is the longest period you have played it for lately? When was the last time you felt motivated to play it?

Only by changing the game, or the rules, will you ever have enough interest to not only play the game, but to enjoy it as well. This is your life. This is your game. And these are your rules.

> *Exercise: Write down the set of rules that you are currently following. If there is any aspect of your life that you do not love then write down the rule that you are currently using to justify your unhappiness. Where does it come from? Also, write a list of rules that you would love to be able to use to govern your life. When you have the two lists then you can start to notice what rules are working for you and what needs to change if you are to live more in alignment with your heart.*

Now that you know that life is just a game, we can look at how you can connect yourself to better people and better outcomes.

Chapter 20

Connect With People Who Can Help

L ooking to navigate the path of your heart involves connection to thoughts and people who make you feel good. When you are truly connected to your heart, you will attract situations and people into your life, sometimes seemingly serendipitously.

Serendipity is luck by accident. Through the cultivation of luck, knowing what you believe in, and using your emotions to guide you, you can connect to all of the right people and situations to create flow in your life.

Get help.

If you are not yet feeling good, get help. This is the most important part of the journey beyond loving yourself enough to believe that you deserve to be happier. Ask, learn, invest, be bold and trust yourself. On my journey to help myself I have spent around £100,000 to date. Whilst most of the people I knew were accumulating material assets, which often caused them stress and sometimes induced severe depression and suicidal urges, I was investing in myself, using the rest of my money to travel overseas for a combined total of about six years.

Financial security became less important to me as I went from expert to expert in order to find what I was looking for. I have been lucky to learn from some wonderful teachers. This has been an investment in myself. If you are not already investing in yourself then what value are you putting on your life? All decisions come at a cost: mine was to prioritise fun at the expense of security. Since I'd witnessed so many people die prematurely as a nurse, this was a risk I was happy to take. I never married, had kids or did just about anything that most people do. Being different and thinking different has been my gift or curse, depending who you ask!

Help yourself.

You would be amazed how many people are out there who would be happy to help you. Not only as professionals but also as friends. My friends have been a fabulous source of support and amazement on my journey. When I have a problem, I am just one phone call away from the help of a friend. Letting go of friends who were not serving me, in order to attract those who do, has been a pivotal part of my process. I always get more clarity and feel more support through running challenges and ideas by my friends.

Get to give.

When you allow yourself to get help graciously from others, you will be able to give more back. So many people become great at helping others and giving selflessly, without truly learning how to receive. If receiving compliments, gifts or opportunities is not easy for you then you reduce your flow of energy. If someone compliments you, thank them. If someone offers you a gift, take it and thank them. If an opportunity presents itself that feels good, go for it. It starts when you believe that you deserve it. If you are helping and giving to others already, then you do deserve a little more magic in your life.

When you learn to receive, you will be better able to give.

In the mid-nineties, J. K. Rowling was a single mum struggling on £70 per week. When her friend, Fiona Wilson, offered to lend her £4,000, she wept with gratitude, wondering how she could ever repay such generosity. It is possible that life created this situation to open her to receiving. Then she was able to give back. In 2001, after much success, J. K. Rowling gave Fiona Wilson her £200,000 flat in Edinburgh.

When you start following what feels good, you will be able to repay all of the people who have helped you on the way. Maybe you will not know where to find these gems in waiting yet, but you can only find them if you look out for them. In this case, you could always help a random stranger. If you have not seen the film *Pay It Forward*, then watch it. This film illustrates wonderfully how one person can positively impact the world.

I have known that my life was one of service since a very young age. I just didn't understand how that would unfold. Your life is one of service too. Whether it is service to your family, work, community, country, planet or universe, you are here to serve. That service can only work when you serve yourself first. This will give you more energy to enjoy your life and maybe even have a little fun along the way.

Who would you just love to build up a relationship with?

Think of everyone that you know and even some that you don't. Who you would like to develop a better relationship with? What opportunities are you looking to attract? Who could help you to do that? What will you offer them? What vision will you sell them?

Maybe you have never even considered contacting big celebrities or world leaders because you do not know why they would possibly want to connect with someone like you. The truth is that if you do not ask the questions then you will never know the answer. Whose rule tells you not to be adventurous? If your vision is big enough you would be surprised what is possible.

When your vision and passion are big enough, you will be able to attract whoever you need in your life.

You may not even know who the people are. Just knowing where you need to go and holding the *feeling* of belief will draw people towards you that can help you. You may well be reading this and thinking that you do not have the vision or passion to take such seemingly drastic action. I am here to tell you that this is possible. You have something that makes you truly unique. When you decide to discover exactly what that is and get passionate about it then people who can help you will be drawn towards you.

This process can be exciting and fun.

Sending letters or emails to someone who you would never have thought it possible to connect with is always a good experience. The worst-case scenario is that nothing happens and they do not reply. But what if they do? One email or letter could change your life in a very positive way indeed.

Be a bit cheeky.

When I set up my first website, back in 2008, I had a 'Contact Us' page on it. I found out the emails for Gordon Brown (then Prime Minister of the UK), David Cameron (then future Prime Minister and leading opposition leader) and Bill Gates. I then put them on my page and told people that they could contact me, Gordon, David or Bill about anything they found on my site, placing all of their emails on the page.

I then sent emails to the three of them to tell them what I had done, saying that whilst I did not expect anyone to be contacting them about anything on my site, I would remove their addresses from my site if they were not happy. This way they had to contact me or allow me to use them on my contact page. I also happened to mention to Gordon and David that I felt that I could help them to reform the National Health Service.

Whilst my email to Gordon Brown kept bouncing back and my message to Bill Gates was never responded to, I did get a couple of nice emails from David Cameron's staff. They were ever so polite and brought a smile to my face. They would be sending my message to the Shadow Health Secretary, whose team also sent me an email.

People like to know how their company and staff are performing.

During my time in the NHS, I became good at writing letters of complaint. The degree of nonsense that I was expected to endure made this a necessary evil. However, when I left the NHS I stopped complaining so often and started writing thank you letters to companies when one of their staff gave me good service. This put me in touch with some very happy, influential businessmen.

It suddenly dawned on me that people were far more likely to write letters of complaint than they were to write about good service. Whenever I received exceptional service, I would compose emails to the companies involved. Each time I received a reply it made me feel good. I just thought of how nice it would be for the staff member to hear from a company's head office to thank them. Seemingly small acts like this can start to change your mood, energy and sense of wellbeing.

Exercise: Write a list of at least five people who you would love to contact, then write to them. Tell them who you are, what your vision is and how you think that knowing you could impact their lives in a positive way. You may even ask them for an interview to find their views on the area that you are passionate about. This is great publicity for them and a good road in for you. If you feel brave and have a number, give them a call.

Also, if you have received good service this week, let the head office of the company know all about it. It's a great way to connect with senior figures in business in a positive way. If not, stay on the lookout until you do get good service, note the name of the employee and then write to the head office.

Feel free to add more than five and to do this exercise regularly. Now for a sprinkling of magic...

Chapter 21

Spread a Bit of Magic

If you have children or nieces/nephews then you will know what it is like to witness magic in the lives of others. The wonder of Christmas and Santa, the tooth fairy and all of the wonderful tales about mythical creatures that do magic things, all add a bit of wonder to life. You may even remember the time when you believed in such things.

By looking to spread magic to the lives of others, you bring more magic to your own life.

Whether it is a phone call to a friend to tell them what a wonderful friend you think that they are or a random donation to somebody less fortunate than you, there are many ways of spreading a little more magic into the lives of others. Making calls to friends who you may not have spoken to for a while is good for the soul.

You never know how life will unfold.

During my ten years of working night shifts as a nurse, I used to love working Christmas Eve night. There was generally a festive feel on the wards, plenty of food and usually less work to do. This suited me very well indeed. When I worked on the acute admission ward, there was usually a Santa outfit in the office. I would wear this for the whole shift, having a laugh with many of the staff and patients.

It was 2am on Christmas morning and the ward was silent as I strolled from room to room, checking on the patients. As I walked into one of the rooms, I had a sense that all was not well with one of the old ladies, Mary.

I went swiftly over to her and soon assessed that she was dead.

This is rarely a good thing for someone who was not expected to die. I told our care assistant to put out the crash call as I grabbed the resuscitation trolley and ran back to the bed. I flattened the bed, removed the pillows, put in an airway, placed the oxygen mask on her face, attached her to a cardiac monitor and started cardiac compressions on her chest as the monitor displayed a flat line.

This continued for a few minutes before the crash team arrived. It was amusing to see their responses at finding Santa doing cardiac compressions on an old lady. They started pumping her full of drugs in an attempt to stimulate her heart into action. After a few tense minutes, an impressive array of atropine and adrenaline, and a few hundred volts of electricity administered via the paddles of the defibrillator, a blip appeared on the cardiac monitor. Mary's heart had decided to beat again.

I stopped the cardiac compressions and stood looking over Mary's face. After a minute or so her eyes opened. I had almost forgotten that I was dressed as Santa and how that must have appeared to someone who had been clinically dead two minutes earlier. Her face was priceless. She clearly didn't know whether she was still alive or dead as she looked me in the eye, grabbed my hand and questioned me: 'Santa?'

'It's OK Mary, you're still alive,' I smiled. 'Merry Christmas.'

There was a pause for a few seconds before she squeezed my hand and smiled back, 'Thank you Santa.'

I let go of her hand, looked at the crash team, who were now smiling too and walked out of the room. The feeling that I had as I did so was nothing short of amazing. I had helped bring a lady back from the dead on Christmas morning. This infused me with a festive spirit, the likes of which I had never felt before.

I decided to change out of my outfit at that point, as I didn't want her to realise that I may not have been the real Santa. Of course, as far as she was concerned I was real, and so was the feeling that we were both left with.

You can create magic.

If you have children then this is easy. Allow yourself to get caught up in their magical world, where infinite possibilities exist, where Santa is real and Angels are there to help them. It is wonderful to entertain a world of wonder. If you are not sure how to do it then consider helping them to perform a random act of kindness. Whatever it is that connects you to that magical feeling, do it.

Exercise: Remember a time when you felt the magic of life. Maybe it was waiting for Santa, opening your gifts or being present at the birth of your child. Whatever it was, remember it until you can feel that magical memory. When you are feeling it, set your intention to attract more of this into your life. You can help yourself by asking yourself: what else would make me feel this way?

When you are ready to attract more magic into your life, you are ready for the final chapter...

Chapter 22

Your Next Step

By now, you probably realise that your self-destruct button led you to this book because you identified with it before you even picked it up. Know for sure that everyone who dies of natural causes and many that don't have had a mental breakdown at some point. The world is more like a lunatic asylum so this is inevitable. Unfortunately for some, it happens too late in life to do anything about it.

Your emotions are your guide to a happier life and you can get more in touch with them by understanding that your body is energetic. Your physical and energetic bodies work in parallel, and most illness, both mental and physical, is because of a failure to integrate and understand how both systems work.

You have had a chance to look at your relationship with the world, with others and with yourself. You know that putting your needs first is the most important thing that you will ever do for your heart. You now understand how your thoughts and language influence your energy and mood, and that all emotions have a positive intention.

We have questioned your beliefs, discussed the healing power that your thoughts have and identified how small changes in your life can make a big difference when they are maintained. Luck has been examined and how you can cultivate more of it. You have been tested in your life and know that you will be again. This is as much a part of your journey as the breakthroughs and amazing moments. One contributes to the other.

You have had a chance to consider and identify what exactly motivates you and how to use this to your advantage. You know how to set your energy space for more favourable outcomes and the different levels of healing. Some people do not heal physically for certain reasons. You now know this and can let go of your need to fix anyone but yourself.

We have looked at how to use your language to get more positive results, and how believing in yourself is essential on your journey. You know that there will be chaos in your life but that time will always make sense of it, when you look for the bigger picture.

You have a dark side. We have looked at how loving your darkest aspects, habits and moments will help you to open up your brighter, lighter, healing potential, freeing you from judgement. This is the foundation of discovering and owning just how incredible you are. You can only do this by focusing your time and energy on your feelings and noticing what makes you happy.

Will you take a leap of faith? By now, you probably know how important this is for you. We know that common sense does not exist and that humour is an essential tool in your life. You have examined your rules for life and know that by changing them you will be better able to connect with the people and situations that align you with your heart's message and desire.

It's over to you.

Only you can help yourself, love yourself and take the required action to tune into and align with the message of your heart. For this reason I cannot promise you that the information in this book will change your life. Only you can do that, by loving yourself enough to do what you need to do in order to feel better.

I have asked you to question everything in this book and in your life and I still encourage you to continue doing this, long after you have finished reading. Only by seeking help and asking yourself better and more powerful questions will you get to where you need to be.

BE-LIeVE.

Be in this moment and live in the now. This is the beginning of the rest of your life. Your past is history and your future is a mystery. You can only be totally alive when you are in the here and now. In order to do this it is important to own the fact that everything in your life has brought you to this point: the good, the bad and the ugly.

If you needed more pain than average to motivate you to find and read this book and take positive action, then that is just as much a part of your heroic adventure as any of the triumphs that await you in the future. And those who caused that pain for you needed to, in order to wake you up. Right now, they are your greatest guides and best friends, especially if they had to do something terrible to you to jolt you out of your discontent.

What is possible and isn't can only be found out by taking action.

You cannot know what will happen in your future. Whilst it is good to have a positive goal to move towards, lose all expectation of how your path will unfold. When you let go of your past and stop formulating possible outcomes for your future, you are free to live in the here and now. This is where your future begins. This is where your key decisions are made. This is where your destiny awaits.

Detach from expectation, be present and listen to your heart.

Allow your path to unfold by just focusing on thoughts, people and things that make you feel good. If something doesn't feel good then change what you are thinking about until you find something that does. Phone a friend, hug someone or access a memory that makes you feel better. How you feel is a result of what you think. You are the judge. You decide what cases are open and closed. You have the power to change the moment that you believe you deserve better. Ultimately, you serve nobody by staying in a state of unhappiness.

Know when you are losing the plot.

Two monks were walking by a river one day, when a woman asked them if one of them could help her across the river. It was against their holy vow to have contact with a woman. Faced with the dilemma there was a brief pause. Both monks considered the request and eventually one of them smiled and agreed to help. He lifted the woman and walked her across the river, before returning to his fellow monk. They then continued their walk.

A few hours later, unable to contain his frustration at the other monk's broken vow, the second monk asked, 'Why did you carry a woman across the river when you know it is against our holy vow?'

The other monk looked at his friend, smiled and said, 'I did it because it felt like the right thing to do, and I put her down several hours ago. However, it appears that you have been carrying her ever since.'

This little fable illustrates wonderfully how changing life's rules in alignment with what feels right for you can work wonders, even when others will judge you for it. After all, whose happiness is the biggest priority in your life? And if it isn't you, are they really happy when you clearly aren't? What goal are you trying to achieve? Or more to the point, whose goal?

Strict adherence to rules and a focus on other people's perceived wrongs can lead to judgement and a heavy burden for you, for a long time. Others will judge you, whatever you do. Other people's judgements can only affect you when you judge others. The result of this paradox is guilt. Guilt and judgement are the two pillars that all roads to your self-destruct button contain. When you become so comfortable in your own skin and love yourself enough, no other people's judgements will matter.

Also, if you feel great about yourself your need to judge others will reduce. This is because you will feel happier. By focusing on your own happiness first, you will feel better and ultimately make more people happy. This happens by just them spending time with you when you are vibrating positive energy.

Life is not always fair.

The bigger your purpose is, the more you are likely to be tested in challenging ways. Nothing can prepare you for life but your faith in your bigger purpose, your belief and intense self-love. Investing in yourself is a very good place to start. Giving without expectation of receiving anything back is also a good life strategy.

I was once struggling at a silent meditation retreat in the hills of Koh Samui, in Thailand. I was in pain, doubt was creeping in and I was starting to find fault in all around me. One day a monk told us a story that changed everything for me. The following story is an adaptation of what I heard, as we were not allowed to speak, read or write during the retreat.

The community in the mountain.

There was once a community in the mountain. It was once a thriving mass of spiritual seekers, who worked for each other and loved each other and all of the surrounding land. They grew their own food, made their own homes and lived off the land. At its busiest there had been 100 people living and working in harmony with the land, the community and the mountain.

Over time, people had started leaving, until there were just six inhabitants left. Nobody knew why.

Brian blamed Joe for his harsh manner with some of the former residents. Joe blamed Paul for his prying questions into the lives of those who moved in.

Paul blamed Steve for his antisocial manner. Steve blamed Betty for her lack of respect for the others and Betty blamed Brian for his sarcastic comments.

As they proceeded with their daily business, there was a feeling of suspicion, despondency and caution.

One day Paul announced he thought they needed the help of a well-known wise man, who lived on the next mountain. He volunteered to go and see if he could get any good advice from him. He trekked for a day to find the wise man and asked him if it would be OK for them to have a chat.

Paul sat down with the wise man and told him their community was dwindling and nobody knew what to do about it. Could he offer them any help?

The wise man sat shaking his head. He did not know how he could help them, apologising to Paul for his wasted journey. As the despondent Paul stood up and went to the door, with his head sunk low, the wise man added, 'One thing I can tell you is one of you has an incredible, powerful gift, which they have not yet revealed, but I'm not sure who it is.'

Paul's jaw dropped. After a pause, he thanked the wise man and went on his way.

Back at the community, Paul gathered the other five members around and told them what the wise man had told him, 'One of you has an amazing, powerful gift you have not yet shown to the rest of the group. Which one of you is it?'

There was a period of silence as each member looked at the other. Nobody appeared to know who it was that had this wonderful gift. Paul wondered who it was, looking around at the others. The person with the gift was clearly not willing to share it just yet. Then he started wondering whether it could be Steve. Although Steve was antisocial, he could be using this to hide his gift. Maybe there was a reason for his behaviour. It made him ask himself some searching questions.

Steve started wondering who it was. Could it be Betty who was covering her incredible, powerful gift? Maybe she had a point with her seeming lack of respect. After all, he rarely listened to what she had to say. He started questioning his opinion of her and wondering whether she was the one with the gift.

Betty began thinking maybe Brian's sarcastic comments were a way to divert the attention from his amazing gift. Maybe he had the gift and he was using sarcasm to point out where the community had gone wrong. Suddenly, she wasn't sure whether it was him or any of the others.

Brian considered that although Joe's comments were harsh there was always a degree of honesty to them. Maybe his true gift was weeding out those who were not right for the community. Enough doubt entered his mind about Joe's possible motives to make him reassess his opinion.

Joe started thinking that even though Paul's questions were a bit personal at times, maybe he just wanted to get to know everyone better. In that moment, he began to wonder whether it could possibly be him who had the gift. He could not be certain either way.

In all of the uncertainty and reassessment of the situation, the six of them started being more polite and more respectful of each other. They worked harder, did more for each other and constantly questioned which one of the others was the one who the wise man had talked about. They smiled more, became more attentive listeners and started performing random acts of kindness to all of the others, because they were not sure who had the gift.

Time passed and still none of them knew which one of the others had the incredible, powerful gift.

Meanwhile, people passing through became intrigued at the levels of support, friendliness and selflessness the small community demonstrated. People who had only intended to pass through during short holidays, were stopping and joining in. Many quit their jobs and lives to join them, as word spread of this wonderful community.

After just a few months, there were hundreds of people living in this community. All of them were working for each other and seemingly magical things were happening. People were finding illness was vanishing, health was returning and the food they grew was some of the best in the world.

Reporters and scientists arrived to get explanations of the things which were happening in this mountain community and many of them stayed. And still, nobody knew which of the six had the incredible, powerful gift.

This community soon received visitors from all over the world who wanted to recreate what they had in their own countries. What was once a group of just six people was changing the way people interacted all over the world. None of them ever found out which one of them had the gift. They were clearly keeping it quiet from the others.

As I struggled with everything in my life, listening to this story brought a tear of gratitude to my eye and helped to make the rest of my stay effortless and highly rewarding. The monk's passion and energy as he told this story opened up something within me. It is my aim for it to open up something within you. Who in your life could be hiding their incredible gift from you, and how will you find out?

I wish you luck and fun on your journey. You never know what's possible when you start being kinder to yourself, believing that you are worth it and changing the world in a positive way, one person at a time. It only takes a smile to start that ripple. And for you to find a reason to smile about.

> *Exercise: If you are not ready now to make the changes to feel happier, get help. Phone the most positive person you know, be brave and tell them that you want to feel better. The journey to feeling happier starts with the desire to want to. A smile right now will get you started.*

You are amazing, even if you don't realise that yet. You are here to have fun. You are here to live your life with passion, energy and flow. Life is not supposed to make sense; the world is a crazy place. Accept that, stop judging yourself and others and simply choose to spend time with people who make you feel better. There are other people out there feeling the same way as you now and want to feel better. Now is your time to find them if you don't already know them.

When you find a reason to truly live, you will feel better, attract better thoughts and people, and improve your life. If you do not yet have your heart's message then make that your focus and trust this process.

In gratitude, from my heart to yours,
Adam.